SWITZERLAND NATIONAL GEOGRAPHIC ROAD ATLAS MAP 2025

THE ULTIMATE TRAVELER'S GUIDE TO SCENIC ALPINE ROUTES, DETAILED ROAD MAPS, HIDDEN GEMS AND ESSENTIAL DRIVING TIPS FOR AN UNFORGETTABLE JOURNEY

STEPHEN STRATFORD

Copyright © 2025 by STEPHEN STRATFORD

All rights reserved.

No part of this publication may be reproduced, distributed, or transmitted in any form or by any means, including photocopying, recording, or other electronic or mechanical methods, without the prior written permission of the publisher, except in the case of brief quotations embodied in critical reviews and certain other noncommercial uses permitted by copyright law

Contents

- Introduction 8
  - Welcome to Switzerland 8
  - Who This Atlas Is For 8
  - How to Use This Book 9
  - Why Switzerland Is Best Explored by Road 10
- Chapter 1 12
  - Switzerland's Road Network & Driving Essentials 12
  - Overview of Swiss Roads 12
  - Traffic Rules & Regulations 14
  - Road Safety Tips for Driving in Switzerland 15
- Chapter 2 18
  - Switzerland's Regions with Detailed Maps 18
  - The Lake Geneva Region (Western Switzerland) 18
  - The Bernese Oberland (Central Switzerland's Alpine Paradise) 19
  - The Valais Region Southwestern Switzerland, Home to the Matterhorn 20
  - Zurich & Northeastern Switzerland Region 21
  - The Ticino Region (Italian Influence) 22
  - The Graubünden Region (Swiss National Park & Alpine Resorts) 23
- Chapter 3 66
  - The Ultimate Road Trip Itineraries 66
  - The Grand Tour of Switzerland 66
  - The Alpine Pass Challenge 67
  - The Lakes & Castles Drive 69
  - The Gastronomic Road Trip 69
- Chapter 4 88
  - Practical Travel Information for Road Trippers 88
  - Best Time to Visit Switzerland for a Road Trip 88
  - Swiss Roadside Assistance & Emergency Numbers 90
  - Accommodation for Road Trippers 91

    Sustainable Travel Tips for Road Trippers 91

Chapter 5 98
    Road Safety & Emergency Preparedness 98

    Winter Driving Essentials 98

    Tunnels & Avalanche Safety 99

    Dealing with Car Troubles 100

Chapter 6 102
    Switzerland's Hidden Gems & Off-the-Beaten-Path Drives 102

    Secret Scenic Routes Breathtaking Roads Away from the Crowds 102

    Fairytale Villages worth a Detour 104

    Local Markets, Historic Inns & Viewpoints 104

Chapter 7 134
    Driving Laws & Regulations for 2025 134

    New Traffic Rules for 2025 134

    Border Crossings & International Driving Rules 135

    Speed Cameras & Fines 136

    Parking Laws & City Restrictions 137

Chapter 8 140
    Conclusion 140

    Final Tips for an Unforgettable Swiss Road Trip 140

    Making the Most of Your Journey 140

    Unforgettable Memories 141

    A Note on Responsible Travel 142

    Official Swiss Travel & Road Information 143

Switzerland

SCAN HERE

HOW TO USE QR CODE

- Open your phone's camera app or download scanner app from play store or apple store
- Point the camera at the QR code for a few seconds (no need to take a photo).
- A link should appear on the display, leading you to the location of the code

Oberhofen Castle

Gruyères

Introduction

Welcome to Switzerland

Switzerland is often described as a storybook destination a land where snow-capped peaks tower over emerald-green valleys, crystal-clear lakes mirror charming alpine villages, and historic cities blend seamlessly with modern innovation. But what truly makes Switzerland unique is its exceptional road network, which allows travelers to experience this breathtaking country at their own pace, stopping wherever the scenery demands admiration.

Whether you're weaving through the winding passes of the Swiss Alps, driving along peaceful lakeside roads, or cruising through culturally rich cities, Switzerland offers an unparalleled driving experience. The country's well-maintained roads, efficient signage, and strict traffic regulations make it one of the safest and most scenic places in the world to explore by car.

This Switzerland National Geographic Road Atlas Map 2025 has been designed with one goal in mind: to help you experience the beauty, culture, and adventure of Switzerland most enjoyably and efficiently as possible. Whether you are planning a short getaway or a multi-week road trip, this book provides detailed maps, expert insights, and essential travel tips to ensure that your journey is smooth, safe, and unforgettable.

Who This Atlas Is For

This atlas is not just a collection of maps it is a comprehensive travel companion tailored for every type of travelers who wants to explore Switzerland by road.

1. Road Trippers & Self-Drive Travelers

If you love the open road, Switzerland is a dream destination. With pristine highways, breathtaking alpine passes, and well-marked scenic routes, the country is designed for those who enjoy the freedom and flexibility of a road trip. This atlas will guide you through must-visit locations, hidden gems, and off-the-beaten-path routes that showcase Switzerland's diversity.

2. Nature Lovers & Outdoor Adventurers

Switzerland's roads offer direct access to majestic mountains, peaceful lakes, and lush valleys. Whether you're planning to hike in the Alps, ski in the best resorts, or camp under the stars, this book will help you find the best routes to national parks, nature reserves, and breathtaking lookout points.

3. Cultural Explorers & History Enthusiasts

Switzerland is more than just landscapes it's a country rich in history, tradition, and cultural diversity. From the medieval streets of Bern to the cosmopolitan flair of Zurich, from the charming lakeside promenades of Geneva to the Italian-influenced towns of Ticino, this guide highlights cultural landmarks, museums, and historical sites worth visiting.

4. Families & Leisure Travelers

For families traveling with kids, this atlas includes family-friendly stops, scenic picnic areas, and travel tips for a stress-free journey. If you prefer a more relaxed pace, we highlight wellness resorts, lakeside retreats, and picturesque villages perfect for a leisurely Swiss escape.

5. Motorists & Driving Enthusiasts

For those who appreciate engineering marvels, Switzerland is home to some of the most iconic roads in the world, including the Furka Pass, Grimsel Pass, and Gotthard Pass. Whether you're driving a classic car, a motorcycle, or a campervan, this book offers detailed road conditions, elevation details, and seasonal driving tips to ensure you get the most out of every mile.

How to Use This Book

This atlas is structured for easy navigation, whether you're planning your trip or searching for information while on the road. Here's how to make the most of it.

1. Understanding the Maps & Legends

Each region has its dedicated map, featuring major highways, scenic routes, and key attractions.

Symbols and map legends will help you quickly identify rest areas, parking spots, viewpoints, petrol stations, and more.

Road classifications are color-coded to distinguish between motorways, main roads, secondary roads, and alpine passes.

2. Planning Your Route

If you're looking for a specific region, head to Chapter 2, which provides an in-depth breakdown of Switzerland's best road trip destinations.

If you want a ready-made itinerary, Chapter 3 offers themed road trips, including an Alpine Pass Challenge, a Lakes & Castles Drive and a Gastronomic Road Trip.

For practical driving tips and regulations, refer to Chapter 1, which covers everything from speed limits to renting a car in Switzerland.

3. Discovering Hidden Gems

While major cities and attractions are covered, we also highlight lesser-known spots where you can escape the crowds and enjoy authentic Swiss experiences.

Look for "Insider Tips" throughout the book where we suggest local favorites, scenic detours, and must-try Swiss delicacies.

4. Staying Safe & Informed

Switzerland is known for its efficient and well-maintained roads, but driving in the Alps comes with challenges. We provide essential road safety tips, including advice for driving in winter, navigating mountain roads, and dealing with sudden weather changes.

We also outline emergency contacts, roadside assistance numbers, and driving etiquette to help you stay prepared.

Why Switzerland Is Best Explored by Road

Switzerland is small but incredibly diverse. Unlike other countries where long distances separate major attractions, Switzerland's compact size allows you to experience dramatic scenery changes in just a few hours. A single day of driving can take you from:

Zurich's vibrant city streets → to the quaint villages of Appenzell → to the snowy peaks of the Engadin Valley

Geneva's cosmopolitan lake front → to the rolling vineyards of Lavaux → to the medieval castles of Montreux.

Lugano's Italian-style piazzas → to the palm lined shores of Locarno → to the rugged alpine roads of Gotthard Pass.

No other mode of travel gives you the same freedom, flexibility, and intimacy with the landscape. Whether you want to linger in a scenic valley, take spontaneous photo stops, or chase the perfect sunset over a mountain ridge, a self-drive journey allows you to experience Switzerland on your terms.

Start Your Journey

Switzerland is waiting for you. Whether you're a first time visitor or a seasoned traveler, this road atlas will be your trusted companion as you explore the country's diverse landscapes, charming cities, and unforgettable roads.

Chapter 1

Switzerland's Road Network & Driving Essentials

Switzerland is a driver's paradise, with its pristine highways, breathtaking scenic byways, and legendary alpine passes. The country's efficient and well-maintained road network makes it one of the best places in Europe for a self-drive adventure. However, driving in Switzerland requires an understanding of road classification traffic regulations, toll systems, and seasonal challenges. This chapter provides everything you need to know about navigating Swiss roads, ensuring a smooth and enjoyable driving experience.

Overview of Swiss Roads

Switzerland's road network is one of the best in the world, designed to accommodate both daily commuters and leisure travelers. Whether you are cruising along high-speed motorways, exploring charming countryside routes, or navigating thrilling mountain passes, you will find the roads in excellent condition, well-signposted, and easy to drive on.

Switzerland's road system can be categorized into

Highways Autobahnen: High-speed roads connecting major cities and regions.

Scenic Byways: Beautiful routes designed for slow, leisurely drives.

Alpine Passes: High-altitude roads offering breathtaking views.

Secondary Roads: Smaller roads that connect villages and remote areas.

Each of these roads offers a unique driving experience, and knowing which routes to take can make all the difference in planning your trip.

Types of Roads in Switzerland

Switzerland's road network is categorized into different types, each serving a specific purpose. Understanding these broad classifications will help you plan your journey effectively.

A. Autobahnen (Motorways/Highways)

Fastest and most direct routes between cities and regions.

Marked with green signs and an "A" followed by a number (e.g., A1, A2).

Toll system in place – you must have a Swiss vignette (road tax sticker) to use them.

Speed limit: 120 km/h (75 mph) unless otherwise posted.

Major Autobahnen in Switzerland:

A1: Connects Geneva, Lausanne, Bern, Zurich, and St. Gallen.

A2: Links Basel to Lugano via Lucerne and the Gotthard Tunnel.

A9: Scenic motorway passing through the Lavaux Vineyard Terraces and Rhône Valley.

B. Hauptstrassen (Main Roads)

Primary roads that connect town's cities and important landmarks.

Identified by blue signs with route numbers (e.g., Route 2, Route 8).

Often run parallel to motorways, providing an alternative for drivers avoiding toll roads.

Speed limit: 80 km/h (50 mph) outside cities, 50 km/h (30 mph) within urban areas.

C. Nebenstrassen (Side Roads & Rural Routes)

Smaller roads connecting villages, countryside areas, and remote locations.

Often narrow and winding, but beautifully scenic.

Usually less traffic, making them ideal for slow travel and sightseeing.

Speed limit: 80 km/h (50 mph) unless otherwise indicated.

D. Alpine Passes (Mountain Roads)

High-altitude roads with hairpin bends, steep inclines, and spectacular views.

Best for experienced drivers – some roads can be challenging, especially in winter.

Many passes are closed from October to May due to snowfall.

Famous Swiss Alpine Passes:

Furka Pass: Featured in the James Bond movie Goldfinger.

Grimsel Pass: Known for lakes, glaciers, and panoramic vistas.

Gotthard Pass: A historical route connecting the north and south.

Traffic Rules & Regulations

Switzerland has strict traffic laws to ensure road safety. Fines for violations are high, so it's important to follow the rules carefully.

A. Speed Limits

Highways (Autobahnen) → 120 km/h (75 mph)

Main Roads (Hauptstrassen) → 80 km/h (50 mph)

Urban Areas → 50 km/h (30 mph)

Residential Zones & School Areas → 30 km/h (19 mph)

B. Right of Way

Priority from the right: At intersections without traffic lights, the vehicle coming from the right has the right of way.

Pedestrian crossings: Always stop for pedestrians at marked crosswalks.

Mountain roads: On steep roads, the vehicle going uphill has priority.

C. Road Signs & Important Laws

Seat belts are mandatory for all passengers.

Using a mobile phone while driving is prohibited unless you have a hands-free system.

Winter tires are highly recommended in snowy conditions (chains may be required on some roads).

Headlights must be on at all times, even during the day.

Drinking & Driving: The legal blood alcohol limit is 0.05%, lower than in many other countries. Penalties for drunk driving are severe.

The Swiss Vignette System (Toll Roads & How to Purchase a Vignette)

Switzerland does not have traditional toll booths on its motorways. Instead, drivers must purchase a vignette (road tax sticker) to use the highways.

A. What is a Vignette?

A mandatory sticker that grants access to Swiss motorways (Autobahnen).

Valid for one calendar year (from January 1st to December 31st).

Costs CHF 40 (~ USD 45).

B. Where to Buy a Vignette

Gas stations post offices, and border crossings.

Online (some websites allow pre-ordering).

Rental cars in Switzerland come with a vignette included.

Driving on the motorway without a vignette? The fine is CHF 200 (~ USD 225) plus the cost of the vignette.

Road Safety Tips for Driving in Switzerland

Switzerland's roads are generally very safe, but conditions can change quickly in the mountains.

Obey Speed Limits: Speed limits are strictly enforced in Switzerland. On highways, the limit is usually 120 km/h (75 mph), while in built-up areas; it's typically 50 km/h (31 mph). Always be mindful of posted signs, as limits can vary in different regions.

Use Seatbelts: Wearing seatbelts is mandatory for all passengers. Ensure that everyone in the vehicle is buckled up, as penalties for not doing so can be significant.

Adhere to Road Signs: Swiss road signs are clear and informative. Take the time to familiarize yourself with them, especially signs indicating priority roads, pedestrian crossings, and prohibition signs.

Drive on the Right: In Switzerland, like many European countries, cars drive on the right side of the road. Familiarize yourself with local driving customs to avoid confusion.

Be Cautious in winter: Switzerland's winter roads can be treacherous due to snow and ice. Equip your vehicle with winter tires and carry snow chains if necessary. Always adjust your driving speed to suit the conditions.

Renting a Car vs. Driving Your Vehicle

If you're traveling to Switzerland from abroad, you have two options:

A. Renting a Car

Most major rental companies are available at airports and city centers.

Insurance is included but check for collision damage waivers.

Cross-border travel may require additional fees.

B. Bringing Your Vehicle

Must have a Swiss vignette if using highways.

A valid insurance certificate and international driving permit (IDP) may be required.

Check vehicle requirements (e.g., winter tires in colder months).

Switzerland offers some of the most spectacular driving experiences in the world, but preparation is key. Whether you're exploring the Alpine passes, cruising along lakeside roads or navigating the historic city streets, understanding the road network, traffic rules, and safety measures will ensure a smooth and unforgettable journey.

Zermatt

Chapter 2

Switzerland's Regions with Detailed Maps

Switzerland is a diverse and breathtaking country that offers something for every traveler. From the serene shores of Lake Geneva to the majestic peaks of the Matterhorn, each region has its own unique charm, history, and scenic drives. Here are majors regions highlighting key cities, the most picturesque road trips and top attractions that every traveler should experience.

The Lake Geneva Region (Western Switzerland)

Key Cities: Geneva, Lausanne, Montreux

The Lake Geneva Region, known as "La Suisse Romande", is the French-speaking part of Switzerland, offering a perfect blend of cosmopolitan cities, vineyard-covered hills, and historic landmarks. The shimmering waters of Lake Geneva are surrounded by charming towns, world-class cultural institutions, and some of Switzerlansd's most scenic drives.

Scenic Drives in the Lake Geneva Region

1. Route du Lac (Lake Geneva Drive)

Route: Geneva → Lausanne → Montreux

A stunning lakeside road trip following the curve of Lake Geneva.

Offers panoramic views of the Alps and the French Riviera across the water.

Stops to make: The medieval town of Nylon, the vineyards of La Côte, and the city of Vevey, where Charlie Chaplin lived.

2. Lavaux Vineyard Terraces Drive

Route: Lausanne → Lavaux Vineyards → Montreux

One of Switzerland's most iconic UNESCO World Heritage Sites.

The drive-through steep terraced vineyards offer breathtaking views of Lake Geneva.

Must-visit: Stop at a local winery to sample world-famous Swiss wines.

3. The Col des Mosses Pass

Route: Aigle → Château-d'Œx → Gstaad

A scenic alpine road connecting Lake Geneva with the Bernese Oberland.

Perfect for nature lovers, with beautiful mountain views and traditional Swiss villages.

Top Attractions in the Lake Geneva Region

Jet d'Eau (Geneva): The city's famous 140m-high water fountain.

Chillon Castle (Montreux): A medieval fortress on the lake's edge.

Olympic Museum (Lausanne): A must-visit for sports fans.

Montreux Jazz Festival: One of the world's greatest music festivals.

The Bernese Oberland (Central Switzerland's Alpine Paradise)

Key Cities & Towns: Interlaken, Grindelwald, Lauterbrunnen

The Bernese Oberland is Switzerland's ultimate alpine escape, home to majestic peaks, deep valleys, and fairytale-like villages. It's one of the most famous regions for outdoor adventures, scenic train rides, and iconic road trips.

Scenic Drives in the Bernese Oberland

1. Golden Pass Route

Route: Montreux → Gstaad → Interlaken

One of Switzerland's most famous scenic routes.

Passes through picturesque Swiss villages, lush valleys, and alpine meadows.

2. Susten Pass

Route: Meiringen → Wassen

A thrilling mountain passes offering unforgettable views of the Swiss Alps.

Open only in summer, it's a favorite for photographers and nature lovers.

3. Grimsel Pass & Grosse Scheidegg

Route: Interlaken → Grimsel Pass → Meiringen

One of Switzerland's most dramatic mountain drives.

Features serpentine roads, glacial lakes, and stunning rock formations.

Top Attractions in the Bernese Oberland

Jungfraujoch (Top of Europe): The highest railway station in Europe.

Trümmelbach Falls: A series of hidden waterfalls inside a mountain.

Schilthorn (Piz Gloria): The famous James Bond revolving restaurant.

The Valais Region Southwestern Switzerland, Home to the Matterhorn

Key Cities: Zermatt, Sion, Brig

The Valais Region is home to Switzerland most famous peak the Matterhorn. This is the place for serious mountain lovers, featuring stunning glaciers, legendary ski resorts, and awe-inspiring high-altitude roads.

Scenic Drives in the Valais Region

1. Furka Pass

Route: Andermatt → Gletsch → Brig

Featured in the James Bond movie "Goldfinger.

Offers jaw-dropping views of the Rhone Glacier.

2. Simplon Pass

Route: Brig → Domodossola (Italy)

A historic mountain road linking Switzerland and Italy.

Provides breathtaking panoramic views and old Napoleonic forts.

3. The Great St. Bernard Pass

Route: Martigny → Aosta (Italy)

One of Europe's oldest passes, used since Roman times.

Offers stunning alpine views and historical monasteries.

Top Attractions in the Valais Region

Matterhorn (Zermatt): Switzerland's most iconic mountain.

Aletsch Glacier: The largest glacier in the Alps.

Gornergrat Railway: A scenic train ride with breathtaking views.

Zurich & Northeastern Switzerland Region

Key Cities: Zurich, St. Gallen, Schaffhausen

Scenic Drives in Zurich & Northeastern Switzerland

1. Grand Tour of Switzerland Route

Route: Zurich → Lucerne → Bern → Interlaken

A comprehensive Swiss road trip covering the country's best highlights.

2. Rhine Falls Drive

Route: Zurich → Schaffhausen → Lake Constance

This leads to Europe's largest waterfall.

Top Attractions in Zurich & Northeastern Switzerland

Bahnhofstrasse Zurich: One of the world's most exclusive shopping streets.

Rhine Falls: The largest waterfall in Europe.

Abbey of St. Gall: A UNESCO-listed historic library.

Swiss National Museum: This museum showcases Switzerland's cultural history through a variety of exhibits, including artifacts, art, and interactive displays.

Kunsthaus Zurich: An art museum featuring a significant collection of Swiss and international art, including works from the middle Ages to contemporary pieces.

Winterthur: This city is known for its vibrant cultural scene, including museums, theaters, and beautiful parks. The Kunst Museum showcases numerous works of art.

Thur River: Offering scenic trails, this river is ideal for relaxing walks, cycling, and even swimming in the summer months. It's a beautiful natural retreat within reach of urban areas.

The Ticino Region (Italian Influence)

Key Cities: Lugano, Bellinzona, Locarno

Scenic Drives in Ticino

1. San Bernardino Pass

A scenic high mountain road connecting the north and south.

2. Bellinzona to Locarno

This route takes you from the capital of Ticino, Bellinzona, known for its impressive castles, to the charming town of Locarno, which sits on the shores of Lake Maggiore

3. Lake Lugano Loop

Starting in Lugano, this drive takes you around the shimmering Lake Lugano, offering panoramic views of the surrounding mountains and the glistening water.

Top Attractions in Ticino

Three Castles of Bellinzona: Stunning medieval fortresses.

Verzasca Dam: Famous for bungee jumping in James Bond's "GoldenEye".

Monte Verità: This historical site near Ascona was once a retreat for artists and philosophers. Today, it serves as a cultural center dedicated to art, nature, and wellness.

The Graubünden Region (Swiss National Park & Alpine Resorts)

Key Cities: St. Moritz, Davos, Chur

Scenic Drives in Graubünden

1. Juller Pass

This ancient trade route links the Engadin valley with the towns to the north. The Julier Pass is famed for its sweeping views and changeable weather, which can reveal a stunning landscape of mountains and valleys.

2. San Bernardino Pass

Connecting the Rhine Valley with the Misox Valley, the San Bernardino Pass boasts a mesmerizing array of views, rich flora, and stunning rock formations.

3. Prasüra Malans

This enchanting drive takes you through vineyards and charming villages, showcasing Graubünden's lesser known beauty.

Top Attractions in Graubünden

Glacier Express Route: The world's most scenic train ride.

Landwasser Viaduct: A stunning railway bridge in the mountains.

Swiss National Park: Switzerland's only national park is located in the Engadine Valley and offers visitors a chance to explore unspoiled nature.

Switzerland is a driver's paradise, with some of the most beautiful road trips in the world. Whether you prefer lakes, mountains, or historic cities, this country has something for everyone.

Geneva

SCAN HERE

HOW TO USE QR CODE

- Open your phone's camera app or download scanner app from play store or apple store
- Point the camera at the QR code for a few seconds (no need to take a photo).
- A link should appear on the display, leading you to the location of the code

Lausanne

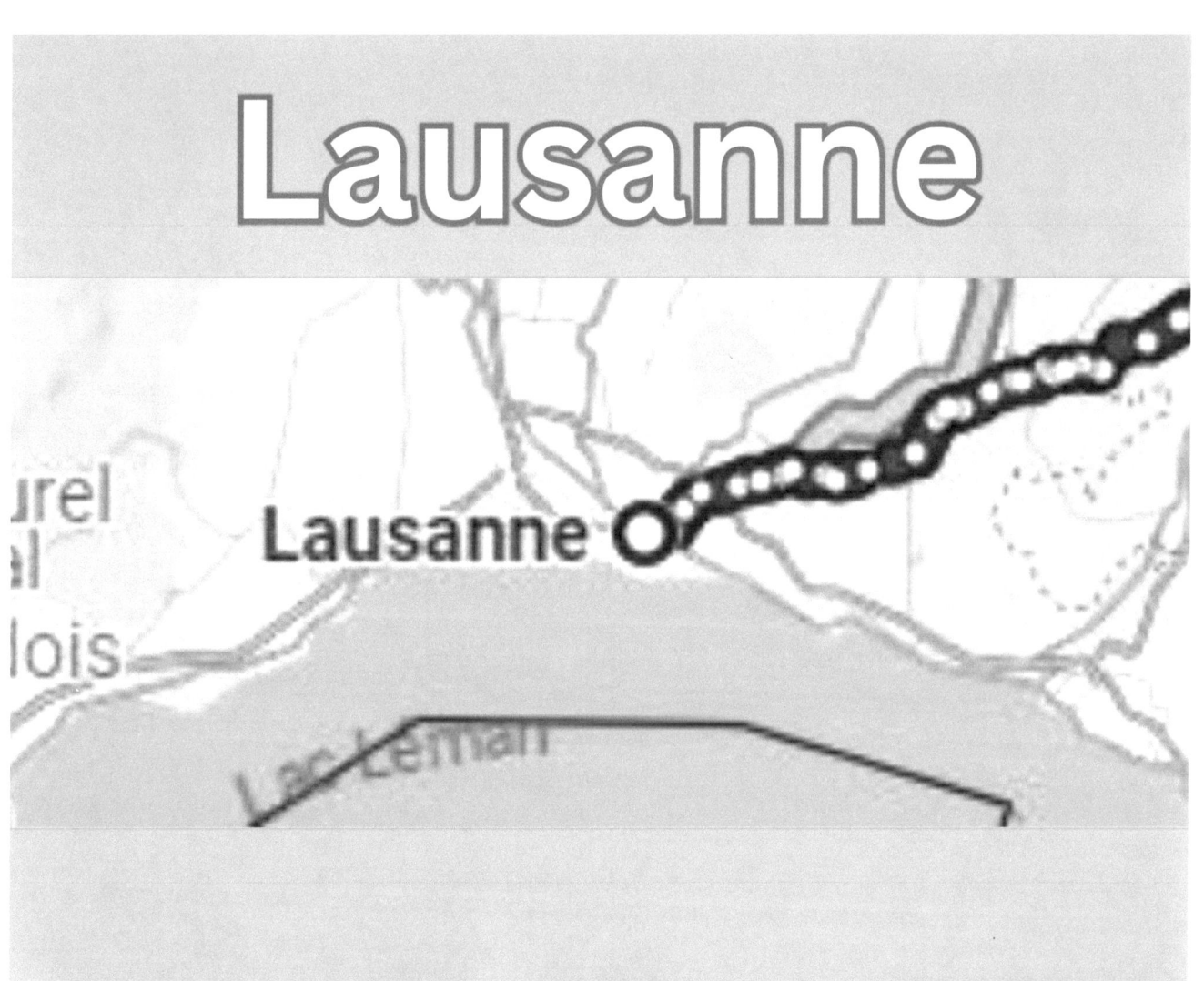

SCAN HERE

HOW TO USE QR CODE

- Open your phone's camera app or download scanner app from play store or apple store
- Point the camera at the QR code for a few seconds (no need to take a photo).
- A link should appear on the display, leading you to the location of the code

Montreux

🚶 37 hr
158 km

SCAN HERE

HOW TO USE QR CODE

- Open your phone's camera app or download scanner app from play store or apple store
- Point the camera at the QR code for a few seconds (no need to take a photo).
- A link should appear on the display, leading you to the location of the code

Lake Geneva

Lavaux Vineyard

Aigle

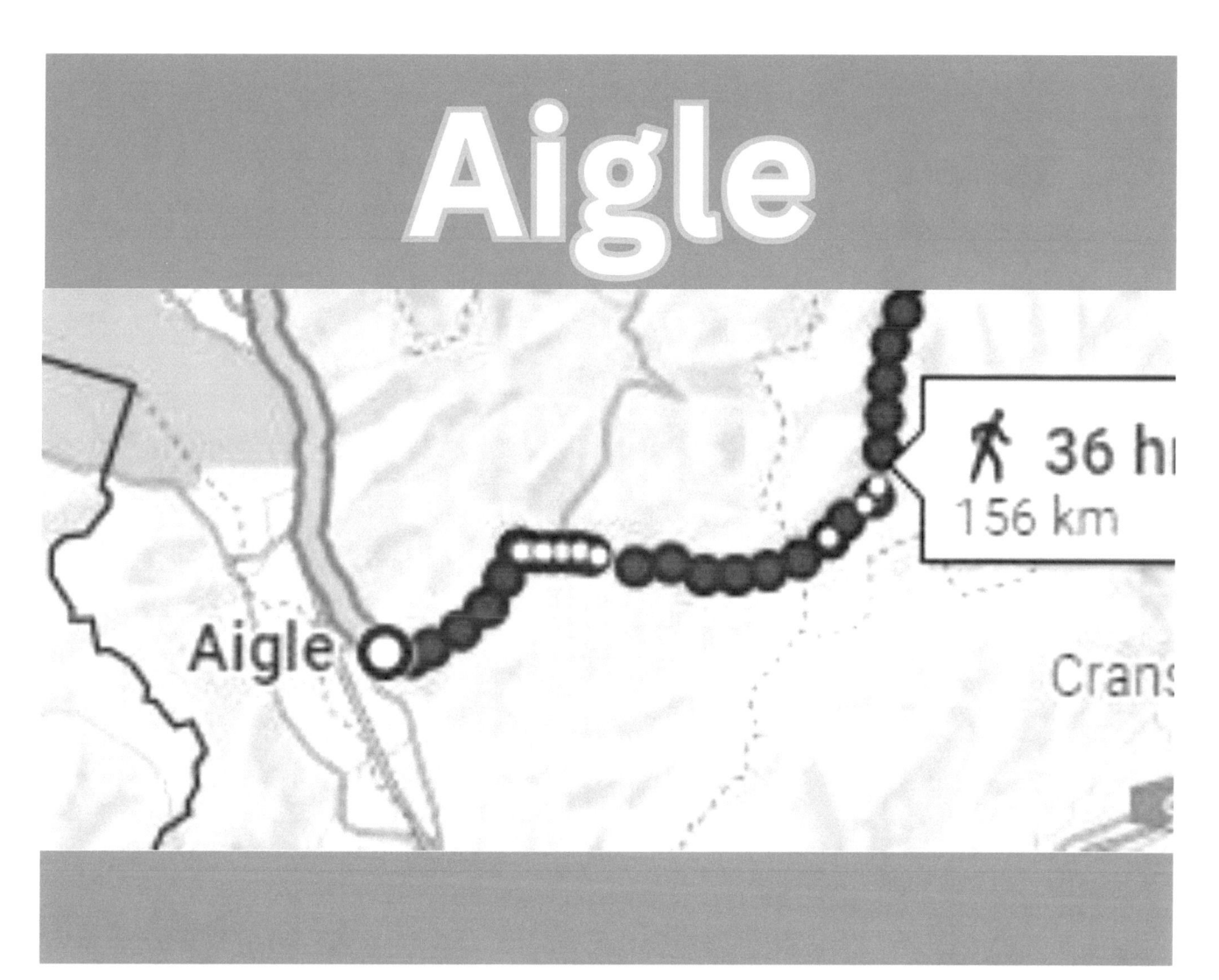

SCAN HERE

HOW TO USE QR CODE

- Open your phone's camera app or download scanner app from play store or apple store
- Point the camera at the QR code for a few seconds (no need to take a photo).
- A link should appear on the display, leading you to the location of the code

29 | Page

Château-d'Oex

SCAN HERE

HOW TO USE QR CODE

- Open your phone's camera app or download scanner app from play store or apple store
- Point the camera at the QR code for a few seconds (no need to take a photo).
- A link should appear on the display, leading you to the location of the code

30 | Page

Gstaad

SCAN HERE

HOW TO USE QR CODE

- Open your phone's camera app or download scanner app from play store or apple store
- Point the camera at the QR code for a few seconds (no need to take a photo).
- A link should appear on the display, leading you to the location of the code

Chillon Castle

The Olympic Museum

Bernese Highlands

SCAN HERE

HOW TO USE QR CODE

- Open your phone's camera app or download scanner app from play store or apple store
- Point the camera at the QR code for a few seconds (no need to take a photo).
- A link should appear on the display, leading you to the location of the code

Interlaken

SCAN HERE

HOW TO USE QR CODE

- Open your phone's camera app or download scanner app from play store or apple store
- Point the camera at the QR code for a few seconds (no need to take a photo).
- A link should appear on the display, leading you to the location of the code

Grindelwald

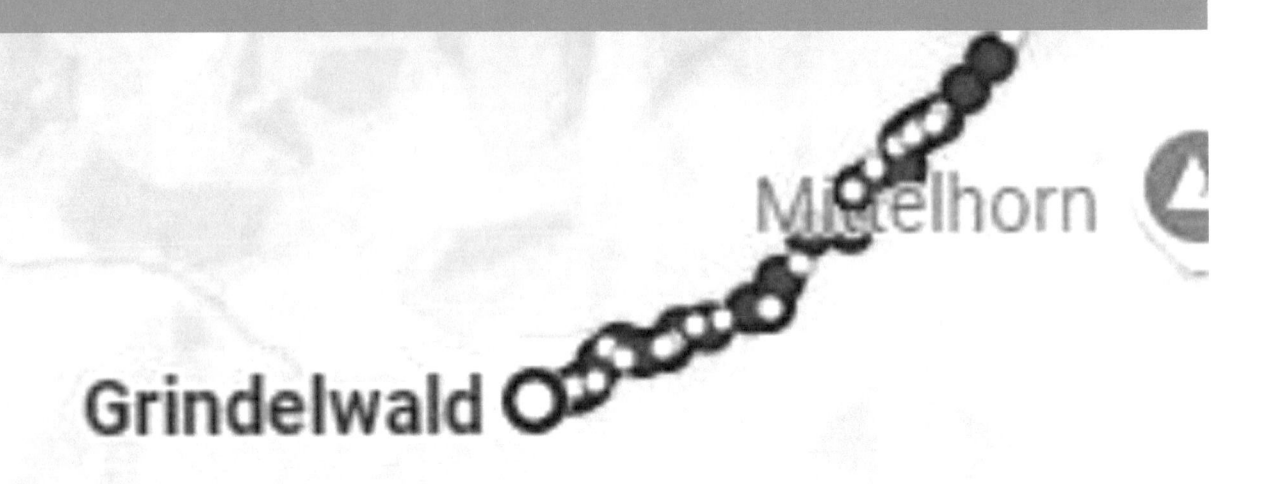

SCAN HERE

HOW TO USE QR CODE

- Open your phone's camera app or download scanner app from play store or apple store
- Point the camera at the QR code for a few seconds (no need to take a photo).
- A link should appear on the display, leading you to the location of the code

Lauterbrunne

Gündlischwand

○ Lauterbrunnen

SCAN HERE

HOW TO USE QR CODE

- Open your phone's camera app or download scanner app from play store or apple store
- Point the camera at the QR code for a few seconds (no need to take a photo).
- A link should appear on the display, leading you to the location of the code

Meiringen

SCAN HERE

HOW TO USE QR CODE

- Open your phone's camera app or download scanner app from play store or apple store
- Point the camera at the QR code for a few seconds (no need to take a photo).
- A link should appear on the display, leading you to the location of the code

Wassen

SCAN HERE

HOW TO USE QR CODE

- Open your phone's camera app or download scanner app from play store or apple store
- Point the camera at the QR code for a few seconds (no need to take a photo).
- A link should appear on the display, leading you to the location of the code

Grimsel Pass

Grosse Scheidegg

Jungfraujoch

Valais

SCAN HERE

HOW TO USE QR CODE

- Open your phone's camera app or download scanner app from play store or apple store
- Point the camera at the QR code for a few seconds (no need to take a photo).
- A link should appear on the display, leading you to the location of the code

Zermatt

🚶 42 hr
176 km

SCAN HERE

HOW TO USE QR CODE

- Open your phone's camera app or download scanner app from play store or apple store
- Point the camera at the QR code for a few seconds (no need to take a photo).
- A link should appear on the display, leading you to the location of the code

Sion

SCAN HERE

HOW TO USE QR CODE

- Open your phone's camera app or download scanner app from play store or apple store
- Point the camera at the QR code for a few seconds (no need to take a photo).
- A link should appear on the display, leading you to the location of the code

Brig

SCAN HERE

HOW TO USE QR CODE

- Open your phone's camera app or download scanner app from play store or apple store
- Point the camera at the QR code for a few seconds (no need to take a photo).
- A link should appear on the display, leading you to the location of the code

46 | Page

Andermatt

SCAN HERE

HOW TO USE QR CODE

- Open your phone's camera app or download scanner app from play store or apple store
- Point the camera at the QR code for a few seconds (no need to take a photo).
- A link should appear on the display, leading you to the location of the code

Gletsch

SCAN HERE

HOW TO USE QR CODE

- Open your phone's camera app or download scanner app from play store or apple store
- Point the camera at the QR code for a few seconds (no need to take a photo).
- A link should appear on the display, leading you to the location of the code

Domodossola

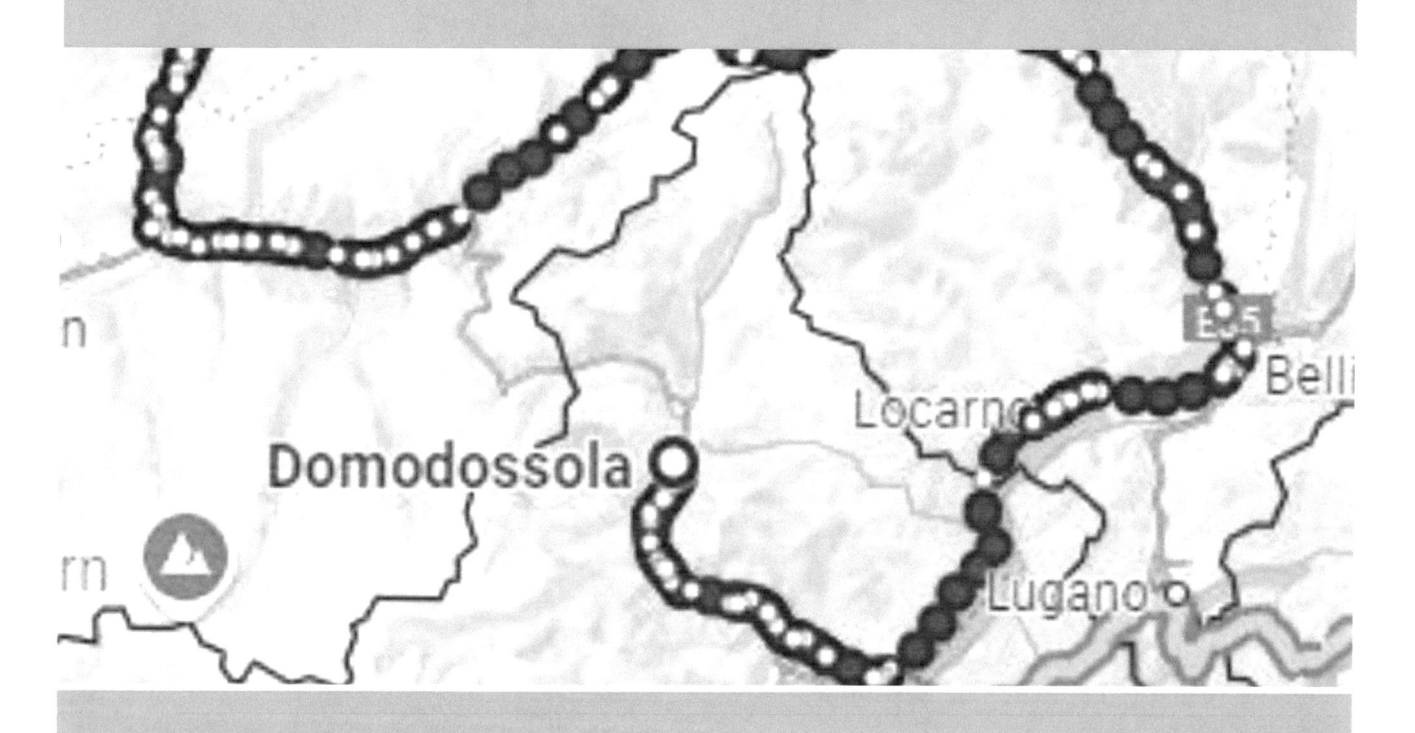

SCAN HERE

HOW TO USE QR CODE

- Open your phone's camera app or download scanner app from play store or apple store
- Point the camera at the QR code for a few seconds (no need to take a photo).
- A link should appear on the display, leading you to the location of the code

Martigny

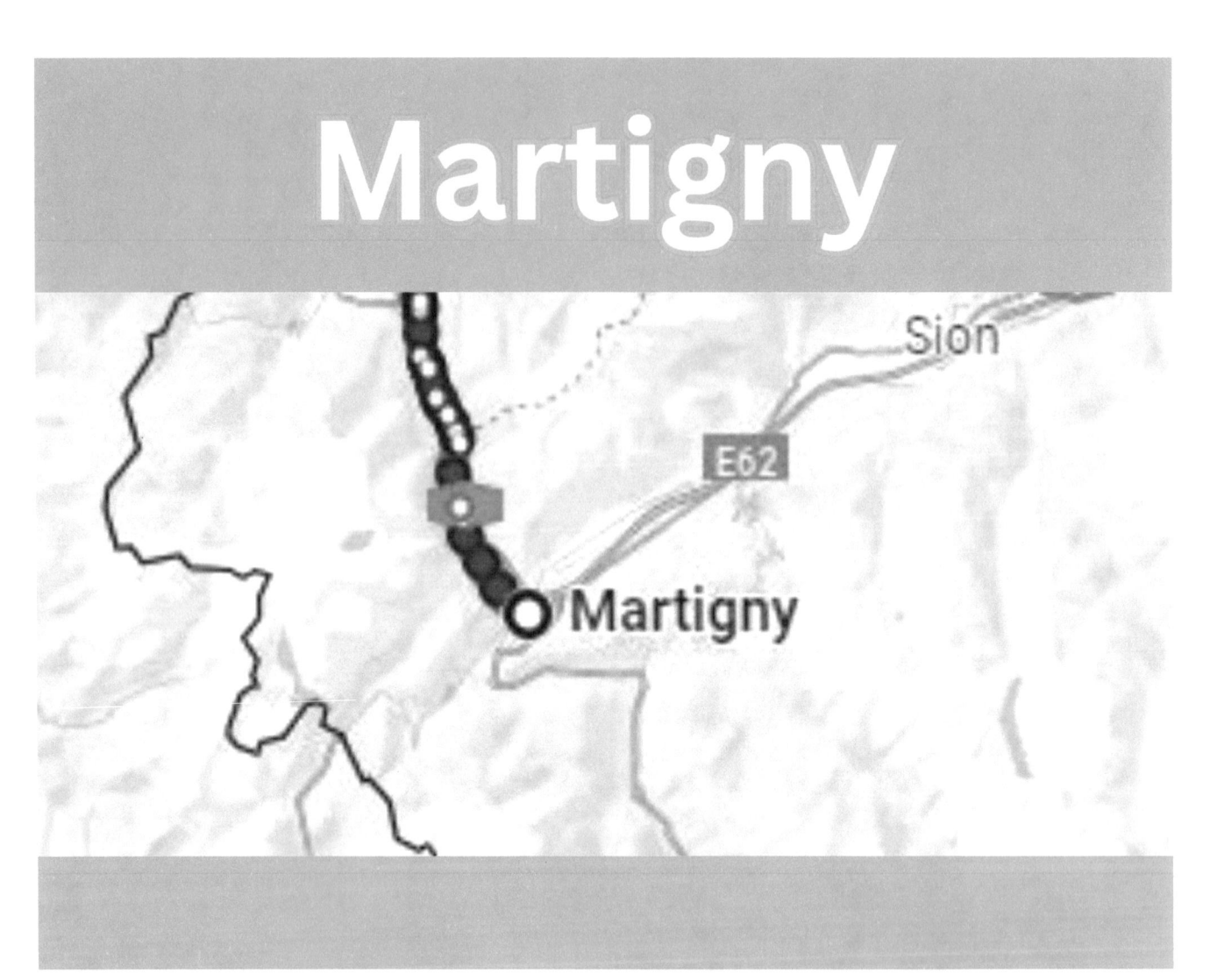

SCAN HERE

HOW TO USE QR CODE

- Open your phone's camera app or download scanner app from play store or apple store
- Point the camera at the QR code for a few seconds (no need to take a photo).
- A link should appear on the display, leading you to the location of the code

Matterhorn

Zürich

20 hr 15 min
4.6 km

SCAN HERE

HOW TO USE QR CODE

- Open your phone's camera app or download scanner app from play store or apple store
- Point the camera at the QR code for a few seconds (no need to take a photo).
- A link should appear on the display, leading you to the location of the code

St Gallen

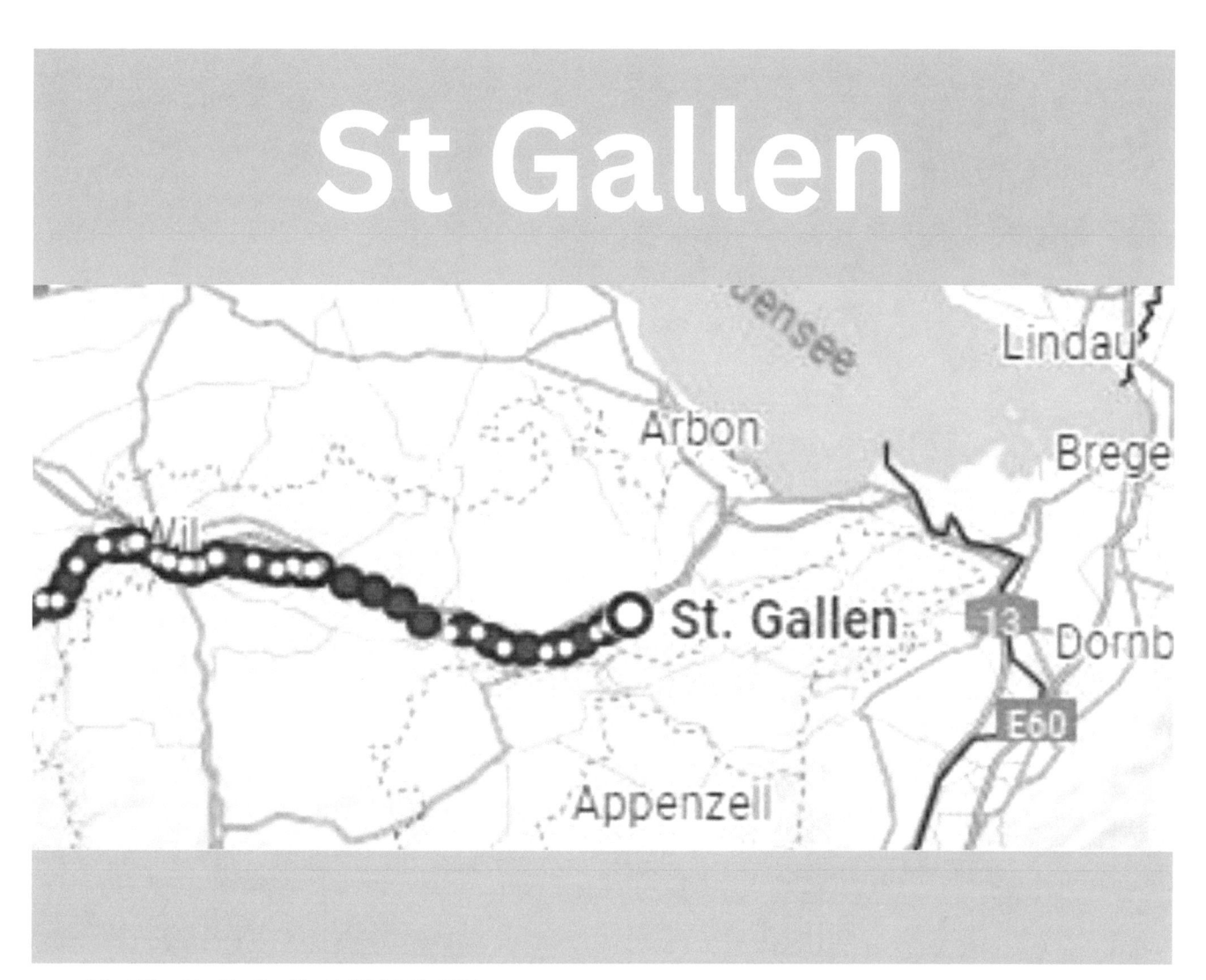

SCAN HERE

HOW TO USE QR CODE

- Open your phone's camera app or download scanner app from play store or apple store
- Point the camera at the QR code for a few seconds (no need to take a photo).
- A link should appear on the display, leading you to the location of the code

Schaffhausen

SCAN HERE

HOW TO USE QR CODE

- Open your phone's camera app or download scanner app from play store or apple store
- Point the camera at the QR code for a few seconds (no need to take a photo).
- A link should appear on the display, leading you to the location of the code

Lucerne

SCAN HERE

HOW TO USE QR CODE

- Open your phone's camera app or download scanner app from play store or apple store
- Point the camera at the QR code for a few seconds (no need to take a photo).
- A link should appear on the display, leading you to the location of the code

bahnhofstrasse

Swiss National Museum

Ticino

SCAN HERE

HOW TO USE QR CODE

- Open your phone's camera app or download scanner app from play store or apple store
- Point the camera at the QR code for a few seconds (no need to take a photo).
- A link should appear on the display, leading you to the location of the code

Lugano

SCAN HERE

HOW TO USE QR CODE

- Open your phone's camera app or download scanner app from play store or apple store
- Point the camera at the QR code for a few seconds (no need to take a photo).
- A link should appear on the display, leading you to the location of the code

Bellinzona

SCAN HERE

HOW TO USE QR CODE

- Open your phone's camera app or download scanner app from play store or apple store
- Point the camera at the QR code for a few seconds (no need to take a photo).
- A link should appear on the display, leading you to the location of the code

Locarno

SCAN HERE

HOW TO USE QR CODE

- Open your phone's camera app or download scanner app from play store or apple store
- Point the camera at the QR code for a few seconds (no need to take a photo).
- A link should appear on the display, leading you to the location of the code

Saint Moritz

SCAN HERE

HOW TO USE QR CODE

- Open your phone's camera app or download scanner app from play store or apple store
- Point the camera at the QR code for a few seconds (no need to take a photo).
- A link should appear on the display, leading you to the location of the code

Monte Verità

Chur

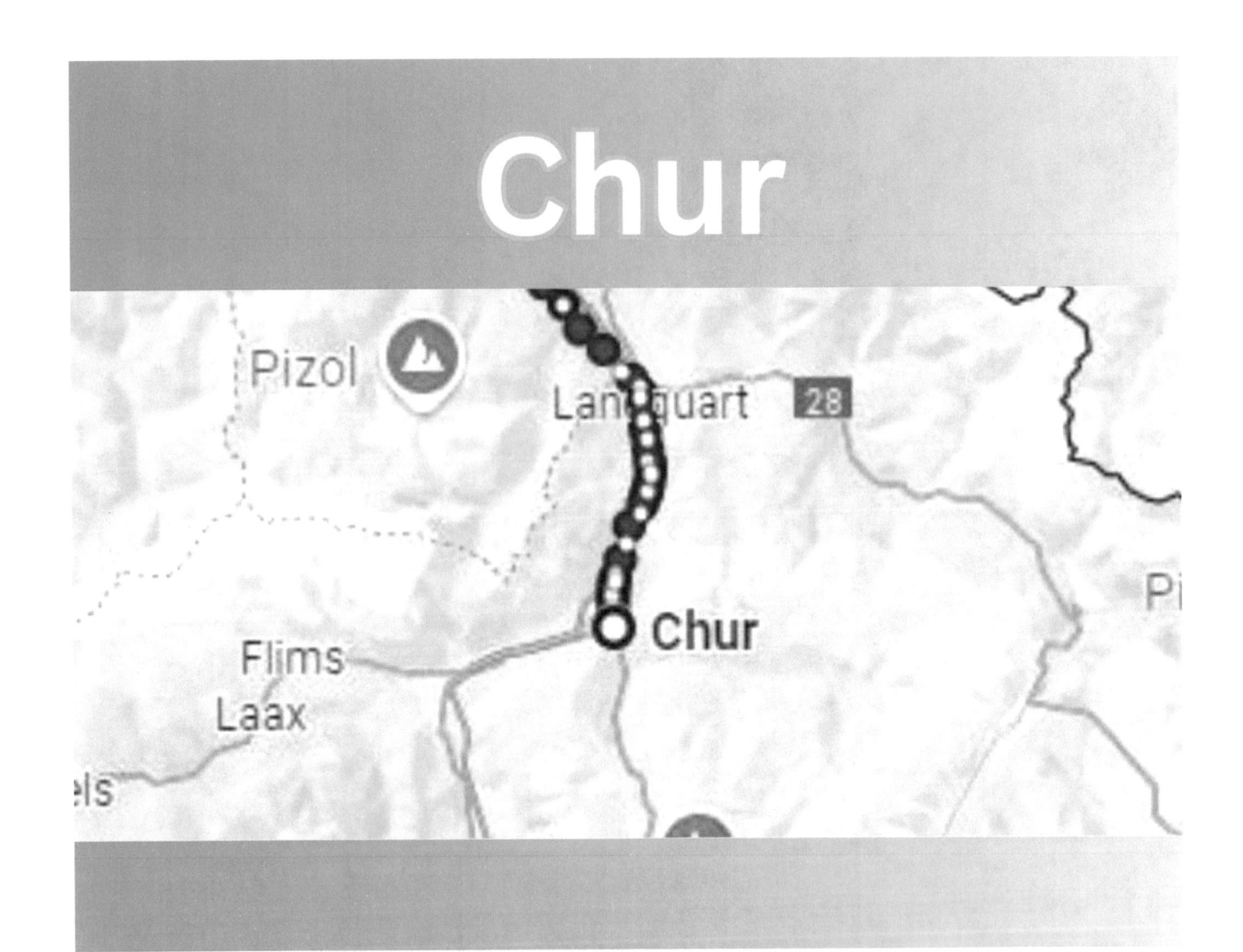

SCAN HERE

HOW TO USE QR CODE

- Open your phone's camera app or download scanner app from play store or apple store
- Point the camera at the QR code for a few seconds (no need to take a photo).
- A link should appear on the display, leading you to the location of the code

Glacier Express

Chapter 3

The Ultimate Road Trip Itineraries

Switzerland is one of the best countries in the world for a road trip adventure. Its well-maintained roads, breathtaking alpine scenery, and charming towns make it a dream destination for travelers who love the open road. Whether you're interested in historic castles, pristine lakes, high mountain passes, or gourmet delights, Switzerland offers a diverse range of road trips that cater to every type of explorer.

This section outlines four unforgettable road trip itineraries that will take you through the most iconic landscapes, cultural gems, and scenic routes in Switzerland.

The Grand Tour of Switzerland

Distance: 1,600 km (994 miles)

Recommended Duration: 7–14 days

Highlights: Cities, lakes, mountains, UNESCO heritage sites

The Grand Tour of Switzerland is the ultimate road trip experience covering the best of the country in one epic journey. This 1,600 km route takes travelers through 12 UNESCO World Heritage Sites, 5 Alpine passes, and 22 lakes while passing through Switzerland's most charming towns and vibrant cities.

Route Overview & Major Stops

Day 1: Zurich → St. Gallen

Explore Zurich's Old Town and Bahnhofstrasse.

Visit the Abbey of St. Gall, home to a UNESCO-listed library.

Day 2: St. Gallen → Appenzell → Vaduz (Liechtenstein)

Enjoy the Appenzell countryside, famous for Swiss cheese.

Take a detour to Liechtenstein and visit Vaduz Castle.

Day 3: Vaduz → Davos → St. Moritz

Drive through the Flüela Pass, a stunning high-mountain road.

Arrive in St. Moritz, one of Switzerland's most luxurious resorts.

Day 4: St. Moritz → Bellinzona → Lugano

Visit the Three Castles of Bellinzona (UNESCO Heritage).

Relax by Lake Lugano, experiencing the Italian charm of Ticino.

Day 5: Lugano → Zermatt

Drive the scenic Simplon Pass into the Valais region.

Take the Gornergrat Railway for unparalleled views of the Matterhorn.

Day 6: Zermatt → Montreux → Lausanne

Tour the Lavaux Vineyard Terraces.

Visit the Château de Chillon on Lake Geneva.

Day 7: Lausanne → Bern → Interlaken

Explore Bern's UNESCO-listed Old Town.

Take a break in Interlaken, the gateway to the Jungfrau region.

Day 8: Interlaken → Lucerne → Zurich

Drive the Brünig Pass to Lucerne, home to the Chapel Bridge.

Return to Zurich, completing the loop of Switzerland.

Best For: Travelers who want to see everything Switzerland has to offer in one grand journey.

The Alpine Pass Challenge

Distance: 700 km (435 miles)

Recommended Duration: 5–7 days

Highlights: High-altitude mountain roads, adrenaline-filled driving, glacier views

Switzerland is home to some of the most thrilling mountain passes in Europe offering hair pin turns, stunning views and a sense of adventure. This challenging road trip is for driving enthusiasts who love the thrill of conquering Switzerland's legendary high altitude roads.

Route Overview & Major Stops

Day 1: Zurich → Grimsel Pass → Furka Pass

Start from Zurich and head south toward Grimsel Pass.

Drive the Furka Pass, featured in James Bond's "Goldfinger."

Day 2: Furka Pass → Susten Pass → Andermatt

Experience the twisting roads of the Susten Pass with panoramic views.

Overnight in Andermatt, a mountain village perfect for relaxation.

Day 3: Andermatt → Gotthard Pass → San Bernardino Pass → Lugano

Travel along the Tremola Road, an old cobblestone section of Gotthard Pass.

Descend into the Italian-speaking region of Ticino.

Day 4: Lugano → Nufenen Pass → Zermatt

Take the scenic Nufenen Pass, one of the highest in Switzerland.

Arrive in Zermatt for views of the Matterhorn.

Day 5: Zermatt → Interlaken → Zurich

Drive back through Bernese Oberland, enjoying views of Lake Thun.

Return to Zurich, completing an exhilarating mountain journey.

Best For: Thrill seekers and experienced drivers who want to conquer Switzerland's most famous high-altitude passes.

The Lakes & Castles Drive

Distance: 600 km (373 miles)

Recommended Duration: 5–7 days

Highlights: Historic castles, tranquil lakes, fairytale scenery

Switzerland is home to some of Europe's most picturesque lakes and enchanting castles. This road trip takes you through the country's most photogenic landscapes, combining history, nature, and romance.

Route Overview & Major Stops

Day 1: Geneva → Chillon Castle → Montreux

Explore Château de Chillon, Switzerland's most famous medieval castle.

Day 2: Montreux → Gruyères Castle → Bern

Visit Gruyères, a fairy-tale castle town famous for cheese.

Day 3: Bern → Thun Castle → Interlaken

Discover Thun Castle, overlooking Lake Thun.

Day 4: Interlaken → Lucerne → Zurich

Visit Château Gütsch, a historic castle-hotel in Lucerne.

Best For: History lovers and romantics looking for charming lakeside scenery.

The Gastronomic Road Trip

Distance: 500 km (311 miles)

Recommended Duration: 5–7 days

Highlights: Swiss cheese, chocolate, and wine tastings

Food is a huge part of Swiss culture, and this road trip is designed for food lovers eager to experience the country's finest culinary traditions.

Route Overview & Major Stops

Day 1: Geneva → Lavaux Vineyards → Lausanne

Taste world-famous Swiss wines in the Lavaux region.

Day 2: Lausanne → Gruyères → Fribourg

Visit the Gruyères Cheese Factory and try fondue.

Day 3: Fribourg → Maison Cailler Chocolate Factory → Bern

Enjoy Swiss chocolate tasting at Cailler, Switzerland's oldest chocolate brand.

Day 4: Bern → Emmental → Zurich

Try Emmental cheese and learn how it's made.

Best For: Food enthusiasts who want to taste the best of Swiss cuisine.

Switzerland offers some of the most diverse and scenic road trips in the world. Whether you prefer historic towns, thrilling mountain drives, or gourmet experiences, there's a perfect itinerary for you.

Appenzell

SCAN HERE

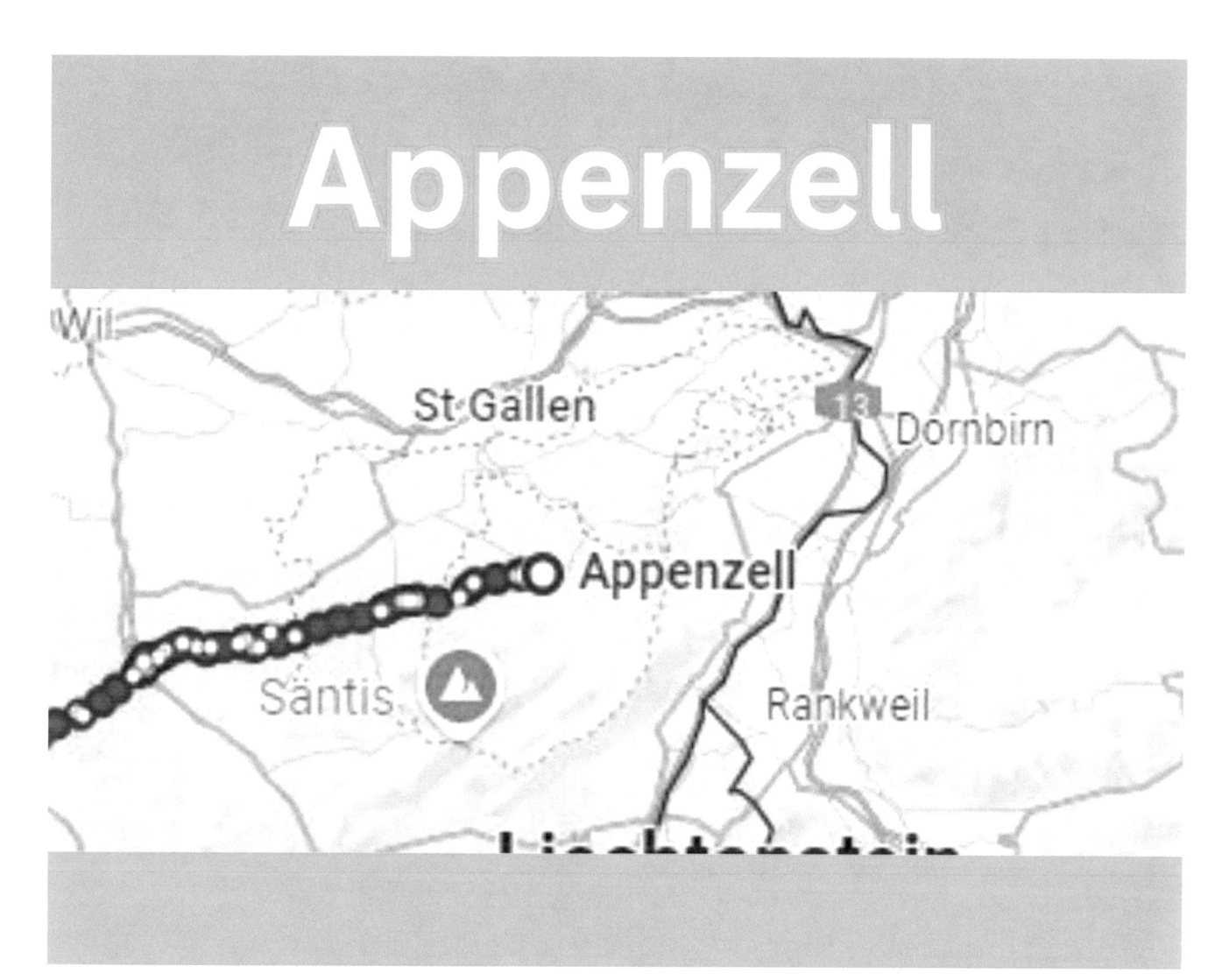

HOW TO USE QR CODE

- Open your phone's camera app or download scanner app from play store or apple store
- Point the camera at the QR code for a few seconds (no need to take a photo).
- A link should appear on the display, leading you to the location of the code

Vaduz

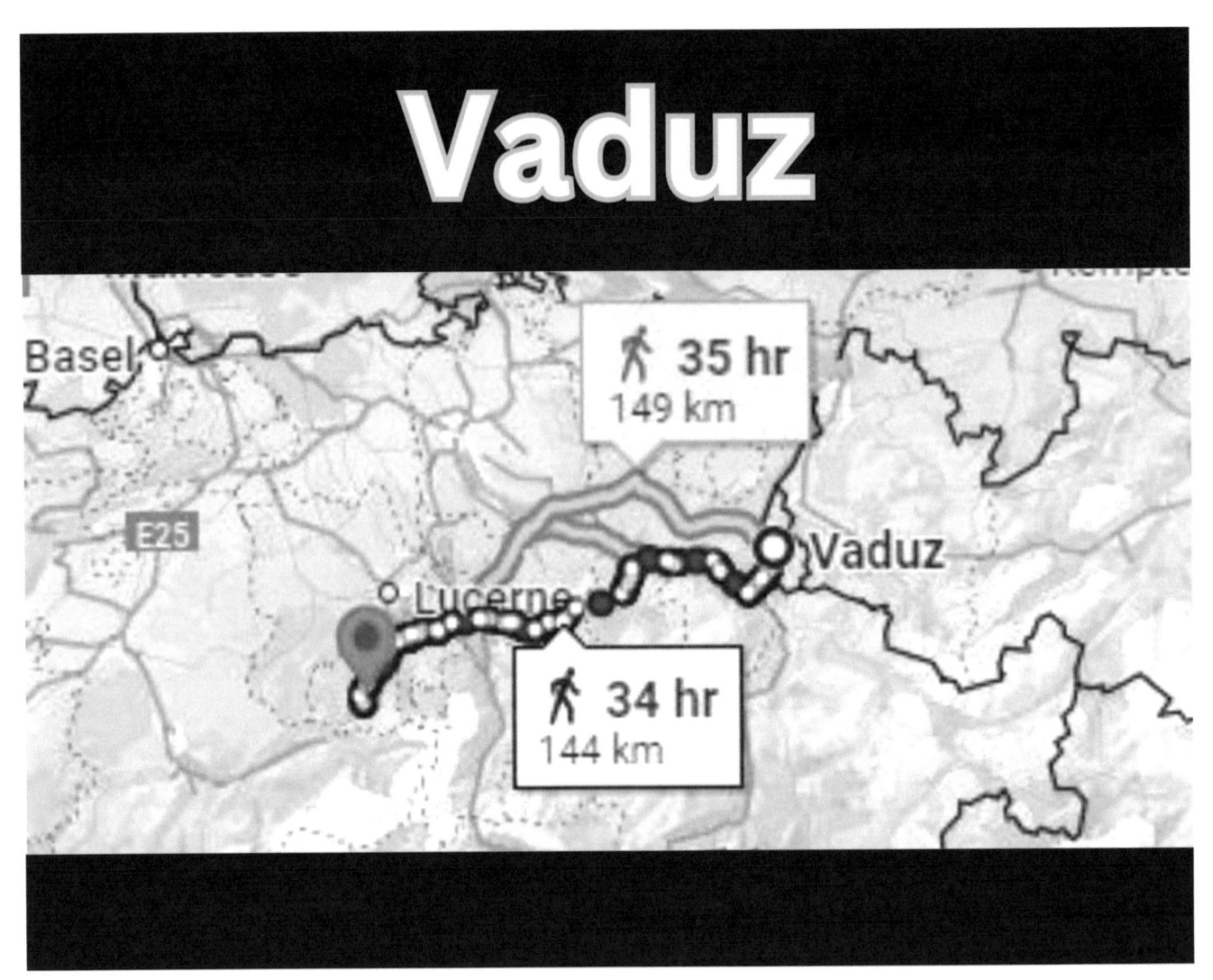

🚶 35 hr
149 km

🚶 34 hr
144 km

SCAN HERE

HOW TO USE QR CODE

- Open your phone's camera app or download scanner app from play store or apple store
- Point the camera at the QR code for a few seconds (no need to take a photo).
- A link should appear on the display, leading you to the location of the code

Vaduz Castle

Flüela Pass

Castles of Bellinzona

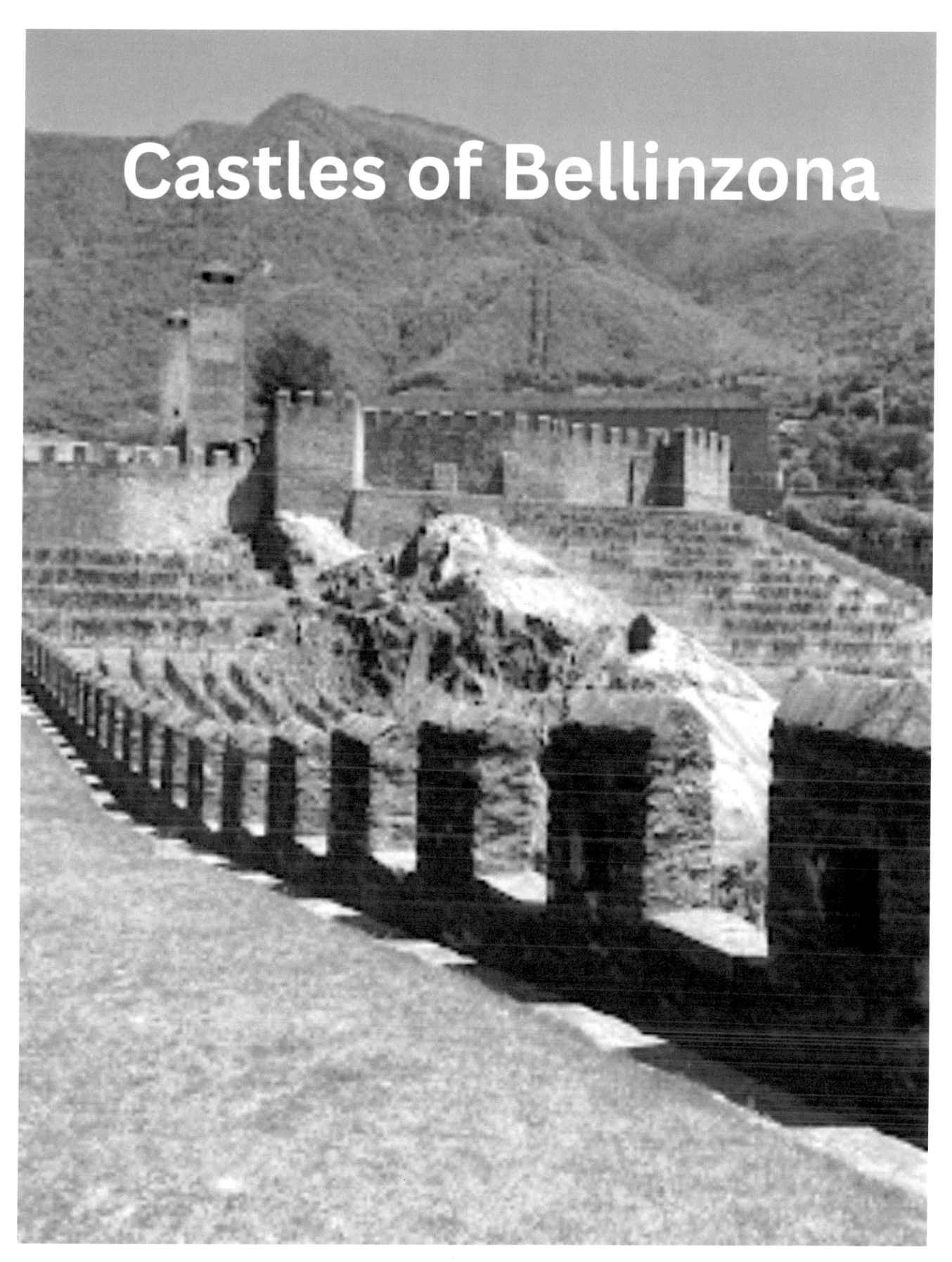

Lake Lugano

Gornergrat Railway

Chapel Bridge

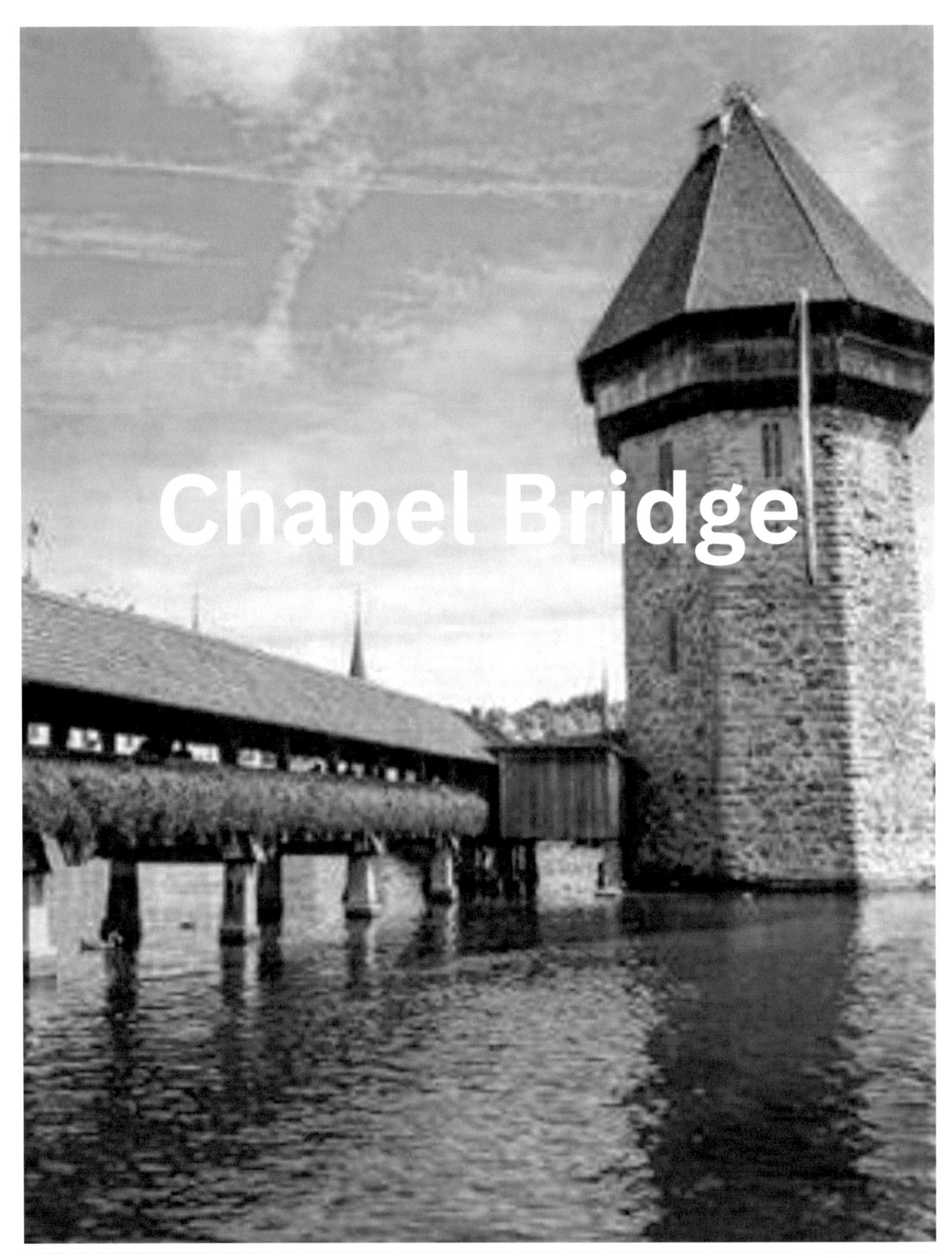

San Bernardino Pass

Nufenen Pass

Lake Thun

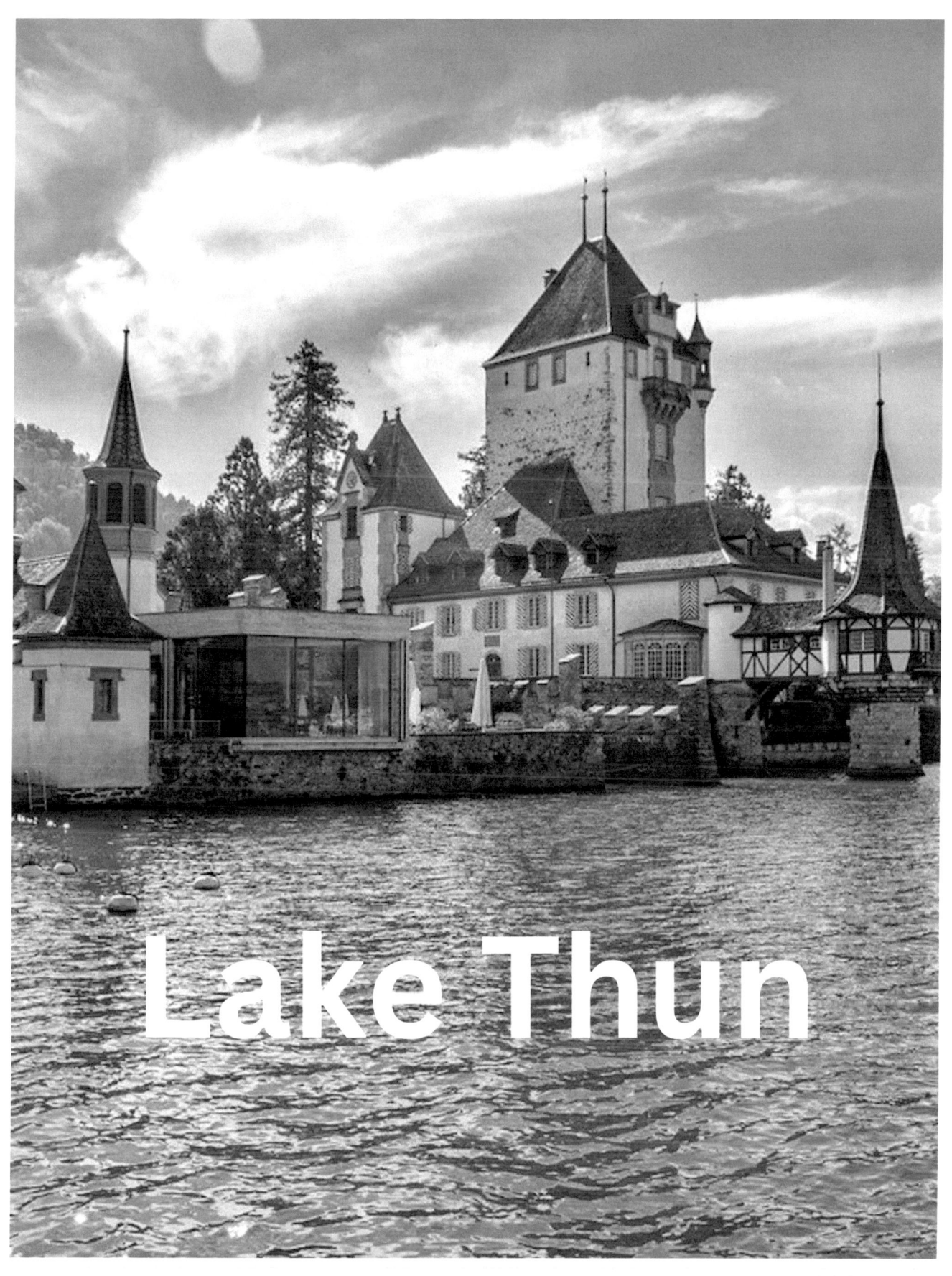

Château de Gruyères

Gruyères

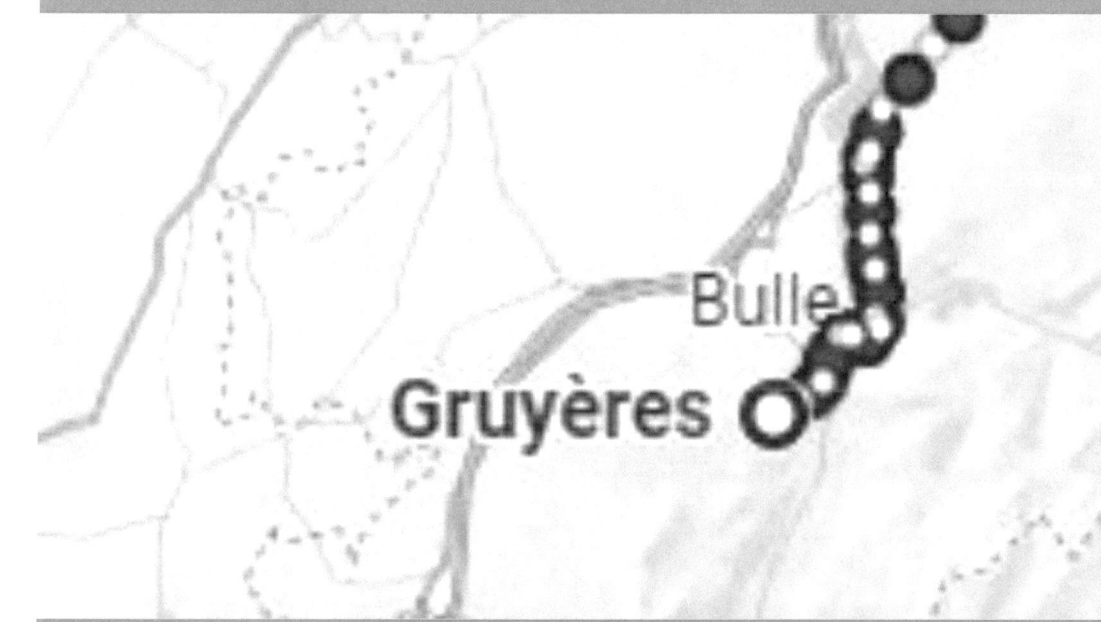

SCAN HERE

HOW TO USE QR CODE

- Open your phone's camera app or download scanner app from play store or apple store
- Point the camera at the QR code for a few seconds (no need to take a photo).
- A link should appear on the display, leading you to the location of the code

Château Gütsch

Fribourg

SCAN HERE

HOW TO USE QR CODE

- Open your phone's camera app or download scanner app from play store or apple store
- Point the camera at the QR code for a few seconds (no need to take a photo).
- A link should appear on the display, leading you to the location of the code

Maison Cailler

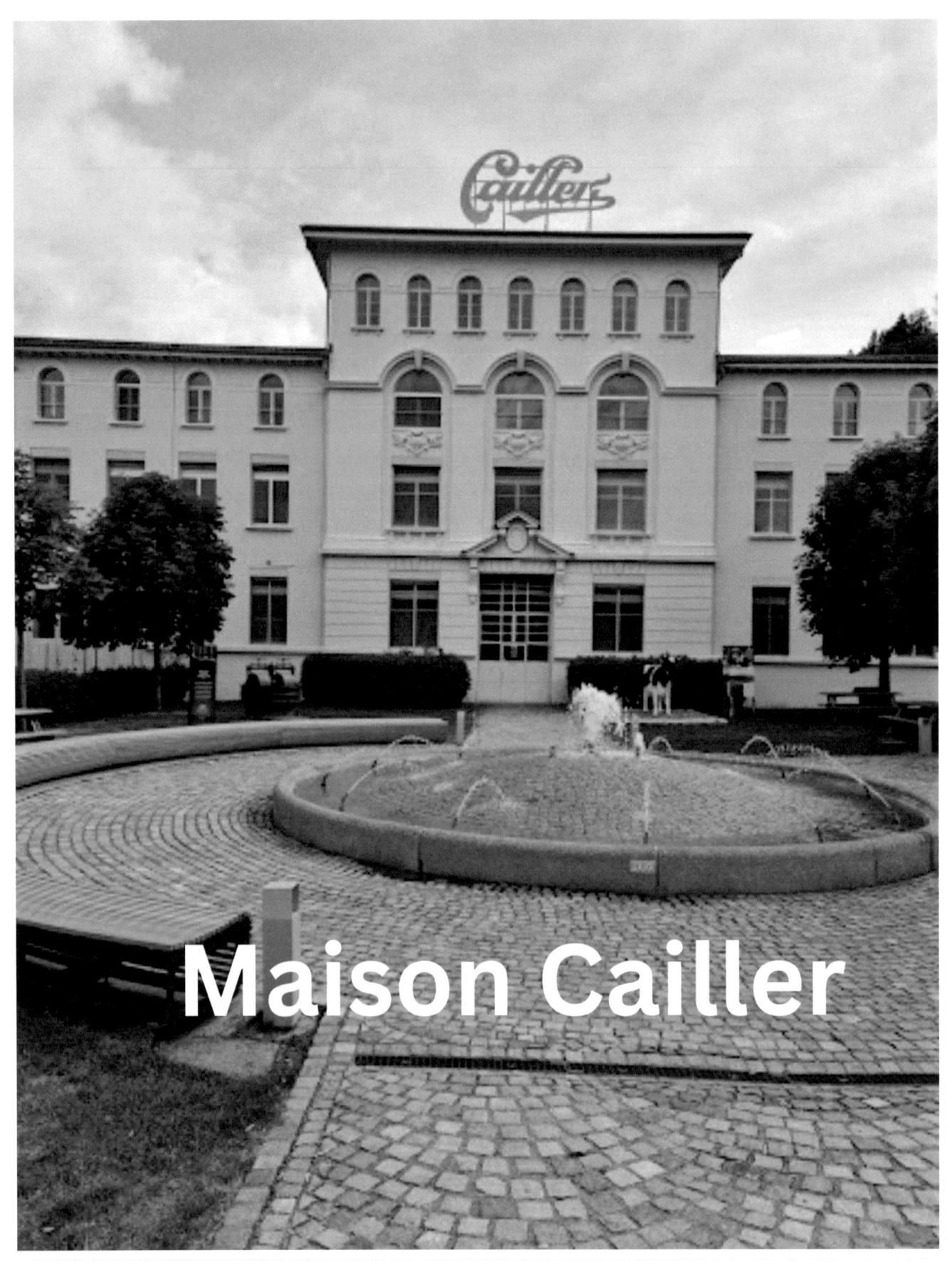

Emmental

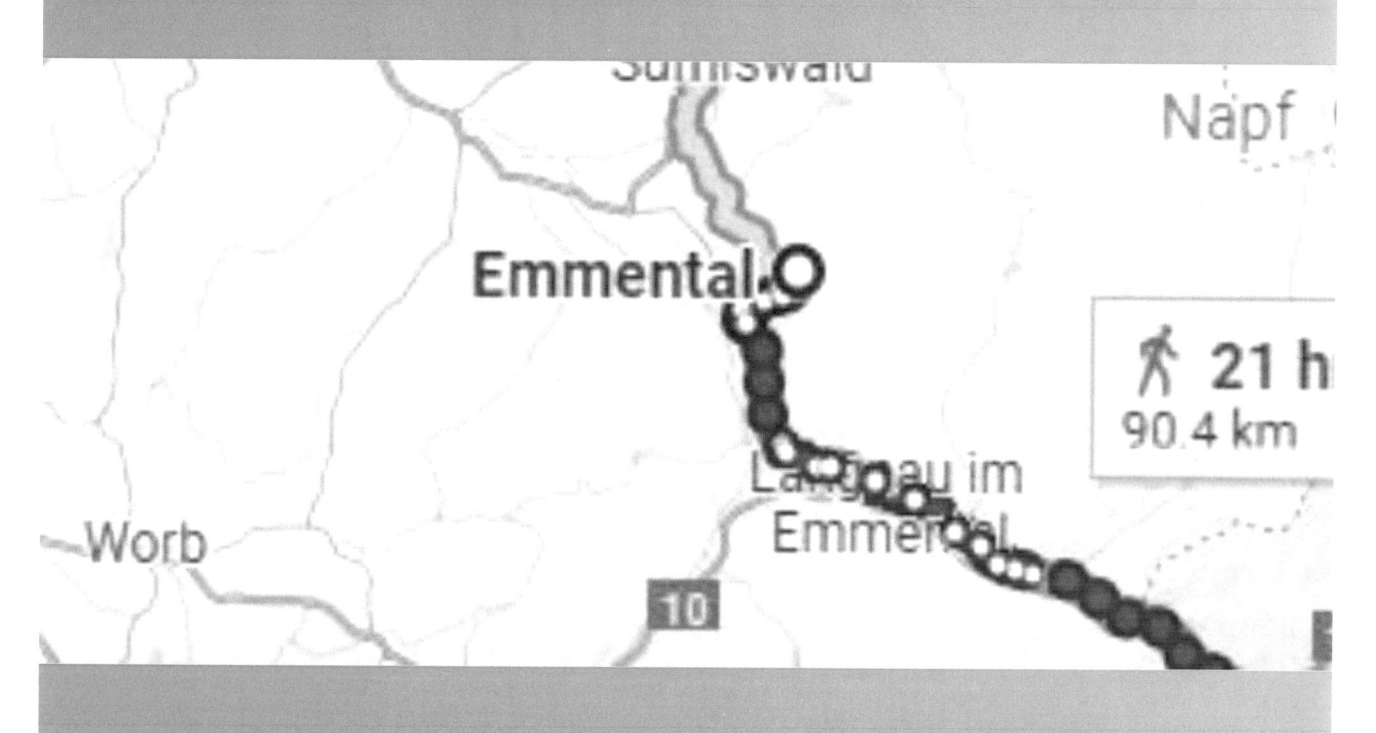

🚶 21 h
90.4 km

SCAN HERE

HOW TO USE QR CODE

- Open your phone's camera app or download scanner app from play store or apple store
- Point the camera at the QR code for a few seconds (no need to take a photo).
- A link should appear on the display, leading you to the location of the code

Chapter 4

Practical Travel Information for Road Trippers

A road trip through Switzerland is a truly unforgettable experience, offering breathtaking scenery, well-maintained roads, and world-class infrastructure. However, to make the most of your journey, it's important to be well-prepared. Here is essential travel information, from the best times to visit and emergency contacts to accommodation options, sustainable travel tips, and useful mobile apps.

Best Time to Visit Switzerland for a Road Trip

Switzerland is a year-round destination, but the best time for a road trip depends on what kind of experience you're looking for.

Spring (March-May)

Pros:

Blooming flowers and lush green landscapes.

Fewer crowds compared to summer.

Lower accommodation prices.

Things to Consider

Some high mountain passes remain closed until late May due to snow.

Weather can be unpredictable, with occasional rain.

Summer (June –August): The Best Time for Road Trips

Pros:

Ideal weather for driving, hiking, and sightseeing.

All mountain passes are open (e.g., Furka Pass, Grimsel Pass, and Gotthard Pass).

Long daylight hours, allow for more exploration.

Things to Consider

Peak tourist season = higher hotel prices and more traffic in popular areas.

Book accommodations in advance, especially in the Alps.

Autumn (September – November): Stunning Fall Colors

Pros:

Beautiful autumn foliage, especially in regions like Valais and Graubünden.

Less crowded, with lower prices compared to summer.

Great time for wine lovers the Lavaux Vineyard region holds harvest festivals.

Things to Consider

Some high-altitude roads start closing by late October due to snowfall.

Days get shorter, so plan your driving hours accordingly.

Winter (December – February) – Best for Snow Enthusiasts

Pros:

Magical winter scenery, perfect for a snowy road trip experience.

Great for combining driving with skiing, snowboarding, or Christmas markets.

Things to Consider

Snow chains or winter tires are mandatory in many areas.

Some high mountain passes close from November to May.

Driving conditions can be challenging, especially in snow and fog.

For the best road trip experience with open mountain passes, warm weather, and long daylight hours, June to September is the ideal time to visit. If you prefer fewer crowds and stunning autumn colors, then September to October is also a great choice.

Swiss Roadside Assistance & Emergency Numbers

While Switzerland has one of the safest road networks in the world, breakdowns and accidents can still happen. Here's what to do in case of an emergency.

Important Emergency Numbers

- Police: 117
- Ambulance: 144
- Fire Brigade: 118
- General European Emergency Number: 112

Roadside Assistance Services in Switzerland

If your vehicle breaks down, contact:

TCS (Touring Club Switzerland): 📞 +41588272222 (24/7 Roadside Assistance)

ACS (Automobile Club of Switzerland): 📞 +41313283111

VCS (Swiss Association for Transport and Environment): 📞 +4158 82715 00

What to Do in Case of a Breakdown

Pull over safely to the right side of the road.

Turn on hazard lights and use a warning triangle (mandatory in Switzerland).

Call for assistance using the numbers above.

If you're on a motorway, use an SOS emergency phone located every 2 km.

Pro Tip: If you're renting a car, check if your rental company provides 24/7 roadside assistance.

What to Do in an Accident

1. Ensure safety firs: Turn on hazard lights and use a warning triangle (mandatory).

2. Check for injuries: Call 144 for medical assistance if needed.

3. Report the accident: Call 117 for police assistance.

Accommodation for Road Trippers

Switzerland offers a wide range of accommodations for road trippers, from luxury hotels to budget-friendly mountain lodges and scenic campsites.

Hotels & Mountain Lodges

Mid-range hotels: Found in cities and towns across Switzerland. Prices range from CHF 100–250 per night.

Luxury hotels: Iconic Swiss hotels such as Badrutt's Palace (St. Moritz) and The Dolder Grand (Zurich).

Mountain lodges & alpine huts: Affordable and scenic, offering stunning views in areas like the Bernese Oberland and Zermatt.

Camping & Campervan Sites

Camping is a great budget-friendly option, with over 400 campsites across Switzerland.

Some of the most beautiful campsites include:

Camping Arolla (Valais): Surrounded by glaciers

TCS Camping Interlaken: Close to Jungfraujoch

Wild camping is restricted, but it's possible in some remote alpine regions.

Airbnb & Farm Stays

Airbnb is available, with chalets and lakeside apartments.

Farm stays offer a unique experience, allowing visitors to stay on traditional Swiss farms.

Sustainable Travel Tips for Road Trippers

Switzerland is a leader in eco-friendly tourism, and Roadtrippers can help reduce their environmental footprint by adopting sustainable travel habits.

Drive an electric or hybrid vehicle.

Switzerland has a well developed EV charging network with over 5,000 charging stations.

EV-friendly routes include: the Grand Tour of Switzerland's electric version, which follows a network of charging stations.

Choose eco-friendly accommodations

Many hotels in Switzerland have sustainability certifications (e.g, Green Globe, Swisstainable).

Respect nature & minimize waste.

Stick to designated roads and parking areas.

Reduce plastic use by refilling water bottles at Swiss fountains.

Useful Mobile Apps for Road Trips in Switzerland

Before hitting the road, download these must-have apps for a smooth journey.

Fuel & EV Charging

Plugsurfing: Shows charging stations for electric vehicles.

Petrol Stations Switzerland: Helps locate the cheapest fuel stations.

Parking & Traffic Info

Parking pay: Pay for parking digitally in Swiss cities.

Viasuisse: Live traffic conditions, road closures, and accident reports.

Weather & Road Conditions

MeteoSwiss: Switzerland's most accurate weather app.

TCS Info: Updates on road conditions, mountain pass closures, and accidents.

A successful Swiss road trip requires careful planning, but with the right information, it can be one of the most rewarding travel experiences in the world.

Zermatt

SCAN HERE

HOW TO USE QR CODE

- Open your phone's camera app or download scanner app from play store or apple store
- Point the camera at the QR code for a few seconds (no need to take a photo).
- A link should appear on the display, leading you to the location of the code

Badrutt's Palace Hotel St. Moritz

The Dolder Grand

Camping Arolla

TCS Camping Interlaken

Chapter 5

Road Safety & Emergency Preparedness

Switzerland's breathtaking landscapes make it one of the most scenic places to drive, but its high mountain roads, tunnels, and winter conditions present unique challenges. Proper preparation and awareness are essential to ensure a safe and enjoyable road trip. This section covers winter driving tips, tunnel and avalanche safety, emergency procedures, and how to handle car troubles while on the road.

Winter Driving Essentials

Switzerland's harsh winters bring heavy snowfall, icy roads, and fog, making winter driving more challenging, especially in alpine regions. If you plan to drive in winter (November-March), be well-prepared.

1. Snow Tires: Mandatory in Winter Conditions

Snow tires (winter tires) are highly recommended from October to April and mandatory in some areas during extreme weather.

If an accident occurs and you don't have winter tires, you may be held liable for damages.

Look for the snowflake symbol on tires, which indicates they are suitable for winter driving.

2. Snow Chains: Essential for Mountain Roads

Snow chains are required on certain roads, especially in the Alps.

Roads, where chains are mandatory, are marked with a blue circular sign with a tire and chain icon.

Even with snow tires, you may still need chains on steep, icy roads.

3. Driving on Icy Roads: Key Safety Tips

Drive slowly and avoid sudden braking or acceleration.

Use a higher gear when driving uphill to prevent wheel spin.

Maintain extra distance between vehicles, as stopping distances increase on ice.

Avoid cruise control; it can make driving unsafe on slippery surfaces.

4. Fog & Poor Visibility

Fog is common in valleys and lakeside areas in winter.

Use fog lights and reduce speed if visibility is low.

Stay alert for black ice (invisible ice patches) on bridges and shaded areas.

Tunnels & Avalanche Safety

Switzerland has some of the longest tunnels in the world, ensuring year-round connectivity through the mountains. However, tunnel safety and avalanche precautions are crucial when driving in alpine regions.

Major Road Tunnels in Switzerland

Gotthard Tunnel (16.9km /10.5 miles) – Connects north & south Switzerland.

Lötschberg Tunnel (14.6 km / 9.1 miles) – A railway tunnel where cars can be transported by train.

San Bernardino Tunnel (6.6 km / 4.1 miles) – Key link between Graubünden and Ticino.

Tunnel Safety Tips

Turn on headlights before entering (it's mandatory).

Maintain at least 2 seconds of distance from the vehicle ahead.

Stay in your lane-do not change lanes inside tunnels.

If traffic stops, leave a gap of 5 meters (16 feet) between cars.

What to Do in a Tunnel Emergency

If your car breaks down, turn on hazard lights and use an emergency phone.

If there is a fire, evacuate immediately via the marked exits.

Do not turn around or reverse-stay in your lane and wait for instructions.

Avalanche Safety on Alpine Roads

Some mountain roads are at risk of avalanches in winter (e.g., Furka Pass, Simplon Pass).

Check road conditions before departure (use the TCS app or Swiss road info websites).

If an avalanche occurs nearby, stay inside your vehicle and wait for rescue teams.

Dealing with Car Troubles

Breakdowns can happen, even with a well-maintained car. Here's what to do if your vehicle breaks down on Swiss roads.

If Your Car Breaks Down

Move to the right side of the road and turn on the hazard lights.

Use a warning triangle (place it 50 meters behind the car on normal roads, and 100 meters on highways).

Call roadside assistance

TCS (Touring Club Switzerland): 📞 +41 58 8272222

ACS (Automobile Club of Switzerland): 📞 +41 31328 3111

If on a motorway, do not walk along the road—use the SOS emergency phone.

Towing Services & Insurance

Most rental cars include basic breakdown assistance but check your coverage before driving.

If you own the vehicle, car insurance should include towing assistance.

Towing is expensive in Switzerland costs can start at CHF 300+ for motorway assistance.

Pro Tip: If you're renting a car, ask the rental company about their roadside assistance policy.

Emergency Kit Essentials

Preparing for potential troubles means packing an effective emergency kit. **Here's what you should include**

First Aid Kit: Always be prepared for minor injuries.

Reflective Triangles and Road Flares: These are essential for warning oncoming traffic if your car becomes immobilized.

Basic Tools: A set of wrenches, screwdrivers, and pliers can help with minor repairs.

Flashlight with Extra Batteries: Useful for nighttime emergencies.

Blanket and Warm Clothes: Essential for keeping warm in emergencies, especially in the colder months.

Finding nearby Resources

Having a roadmap or access to a GPS can greatly assist in locating the nearest service stations or mechanics. Familiarize yourself with the layout of Swiss roads and potential repair shops along your route. Knowing where you can find help in advance can save time and stress in an emergency.

Final Road Safety Tips for Switzerland

Always check weather conditions before driving, especially in winter.

Plan fuel stops in advance some mountain roads have limited fuel stations.

Keep emergency gear in the car, including a flashlight, first-aid kit, and warm clothing.

Respect road signs and speed limits—Swiss police enforce strict penalties.

Chapter 6

Switzerland's Hidden Gems & Off-the-Beaten-Path Drives

Switzerland is famous for its iconic scenic routes, such as the Grand Tour of Switzerland and the Alpine Pass Challenge. However, beyond these well-traveled roads lie hidden gems winding backroads, charming villages, and breathtaking viewpoints that most tourists miss.

Here are secret scenic routes, fairytale villages, unique roadside stops, and essential navigation tools to help you plan an unforgettable Swiss road trip away from the crowds.

Secret Scenic Routes Breathtaking Roads Away from the Crowds

While Switzerland's main highways and famous scenic routes attract millions of visitors, some lesser-known roads offer equally stunning landscapes without heavy traffic.

1. The Albula Pass Route (Graubünden): Historic & Dramatic

Route: Tiefencastel → Bergün → La Punt

Best For: History lovers, mountain scenery, railway photography

Highlights

Landwasser Viaduct: An architectural marvel, this towering railway bridge is a UNESCO World Heritage site.

Bergün: picturesque mountain village famous for its railway museum and wooden chalets.

Albula Pass Summit: At 2,315 meters (7,595 ft), enjoy panoramic views of the Alps.

2. The Emmental Valley Drive (Bern): Rolling Green Hills & Cheese Farms

Route: Burgdorf → Trubschachen → Langnau im Emmental → Sumiswald

Best For: Traditional Swiss countryside, cheese lovers

Highlights

Emmental Cheese Factory: Visit the birthplace of Switzerland's famous holey cheese.

Rolling green hills: Classic postcard landscapes with wooden farmhouses.

Trubschachen: Home of the Kambly biscuit factory, where you can sample Swiss cookies.

3. Val Müstair Route (Graubünden): Alpine Bliss Near the Italian Border

Route: Zernez → Müstair → Santa Maria

Best For: Secluded nature, Swiss National Park, cultural heritage

Highlights

Swiss National Park: Drive along its edge, spotting ibex, marmots, and golden eagles.

Benedictine Convent of St. John Müstair: A UNESCO listed monastery with medieval frescoes.

Scenic hairpin roads: One of Switzerland's most dramatic drives.

4. The Jaun Pass (Bernese Oberland): Hidden Alpine Beauty

Route: Boltigen → Jaun → Gruyères

Best For: Alpine views, cycling enthusiasts, cheese tastings

Highlights

Peaceful alternative to busy mountain roads like Grimsel or Susten Pass.

Jaun Waterfall: A mystical waterfall tucked between mountain peaks.

Gruyères: Stop for a cheese fondue in this medieval town.

Fairytale Villages worth a Detour

While cities like Zurich, Lucerne, and Geneva are well-known, Switzerland's charming villages capture the country's true essence. These hidden hamlets are perfect stops on a scenic drive.

1. Guarda (Graubünden): The Village Frozen in Time

What Makes It Special?

A perfectly preserved Engadin village, famous for its painted houses.

Inspiration for the classic Swiss children's book "Schellen-Ursli".

Stunning views of the Lower Engadin Valley.

2. Seltwald (Bernese Oberland): A Lakeside Dream

What Makes It Special?

A peaceful alternative to touristy Interlaken.

Located directly on Lake Brienz offering some of the best reflections in Switzerland.

Featured in the Korean drama "Crash Landing on You", drawing international visitors.

3. Lavertezzo (Ticino): The Emerald Green River Village

What Makes It Special?

Home to the Ponte dei Salti, a famous double-arched stone bridge over turquoise waters.

Perfect for swimming and cliff diving in summer.

Nestled in the Verzasca Valley, surrounded by lush forests.

Local Markets, Historic Inns & Viewpoints

Local Markets worth a Stop

Vevey Market (Lake Geneva Region): Traditional Swiss & French fusion products.

Lugano Farmers' Market (Ticino): The best place to taste fresh Italian-style produce.

Historic Inns for a Cozy Stop

Gasthof Bären (Emmental Valley): A traditional Swiss inn serving homemade rösti.

Hotel Rosenlaui (Bernese Oberland): A historic wooden hotel dating back to 1771.

Best Panoramic Viewpoints on Swiss Roads

Mont Chasseral (Jura Mountains) – Offers aerial-like views over Swiss lakes.

Furka Pass Belvedere – View the Rhône Glacier from a famous curved road.

Road Maps, Route Planners & GPS Navigation

How to Read Swiss Road Maps

Autobahnen (motorways): Marked in green.

Hauptstrassen (main roads): Marked in red.

Nebenstrassen (side roads): Marked in yellow.

Mountain passes: Usually shown with altitude in meters.

Pro Tip: Buy a Michelin or Swiss Mobility road map for a detailed paper backup.

Pre-planned Routes for Different Interests

Family-Friendly Drives

Lake Geneva Picnic Drive: Easy roads with beach stops & vineyards.

Swiss Chocolate Route: Visit Maison Cailler & Lindt Chocolate Factory.

Adventure Routes

Alpine Loop Challenge: Furka, Grimsel & Susten Pass in one trip.

Off-Road Jura Expedition: Explore remote trails near the French border.

Best Drives for Photography Lovers

Golden Hour Drive to Gornergrat: The perfect Matterhorn sunset spot.

Lavaux Vineyard Road: Capture endless vineyard terraces over Lake Geneva.

Using GPS & Offline Navigation

Best Navigation Apps for Swiss Road Trips

Google Maps: Great for general navigation.

Maps.me: Works offline, ideal for remote areas.

Swiss TCS App: Shows live road conditions & closures.

SBB Mobile: Helps you plan car-train transport on tunnels.

Tips for Using GPS and Offline Options

Pre-Download Maps: Before starting your journey, ensure that all necessary maps are downloaded to your device to facilitate smooth navigation.

Regular Updates: Always keep your GPS and offline apps updated to benefit from the latest maps and features.

Familiarize Yourself with Features: Explore functionalities such as route customization, point-of-interest markers, and voice-guided navigation to enhance your travel experience.

Through the use of GPS and offline navigation, discovering the nooks and crannies of Switzerland becomes an enriching adventure, allowing travelers to immerse themselves fully in the breathtaking scenery and vibrant culture.

Switzerland's Best-Kept Road Trip Secrets

Switzerland is full of hidden wonders from secret alpine passes to charming villages untouched by mass tourism. Whether you seek adventure, culture, or relaxation, these off-the-beaten-path drives will make your trip unforgettable.

Tiefencastel

SCAN HERE

HOW TO USE QR CODE

- Open your phone's camera app or download scanner app from play store or apple store
- Point the camera at the QR code for a few seconds (no need to take a photo).
- A link should appear on the display, leading you to the location of the code

Bergün

SCAN HERE

HOW TO USE QR CODE

- Open your phone's camera app or download scanner app from play store or apple store
- Point the camera at the QR code for a few seconds (no need to take a photo).
- A link should appear on the display, leading you to the location of the code

La Punt-Chamues-ch

SCAN HERE

HOW TO USE QR CODE

- Open your phone's camera app or download scanner app from play store or apple store
- Point the camera at the QR code for a few seconds (no need to take a photo).
- A link should appear on the display, leading you to the location of the code

Albula Pass

Emmental

Burgdorf

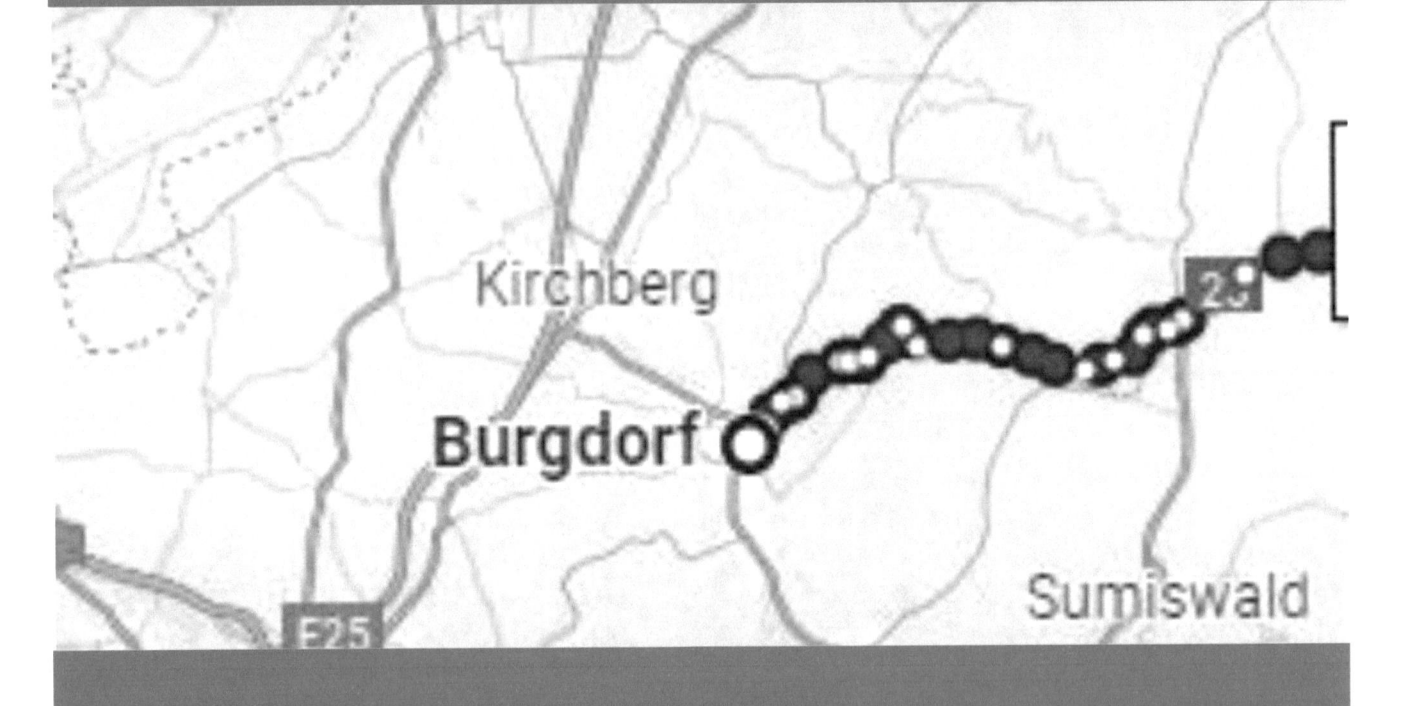

SCAN HERE

HOW TO USE QR CODE

- Open your phone's camera app or download scanner app from play store or apple store
- Point the camera at the QR code for a few seconds (no need to take a photo).
- A link should appear on the display, leading you to the location of the code

Trubschachen

SCAN HERE

HOW TO USE QR CODE

- Open your phone's camera app or download scanner app from play store or apple store
- Point the camera at the QR code for a few seconds (no need to take a photo).
- A link should appear on the display, leading you to the location of the code

Langnau im Emmental

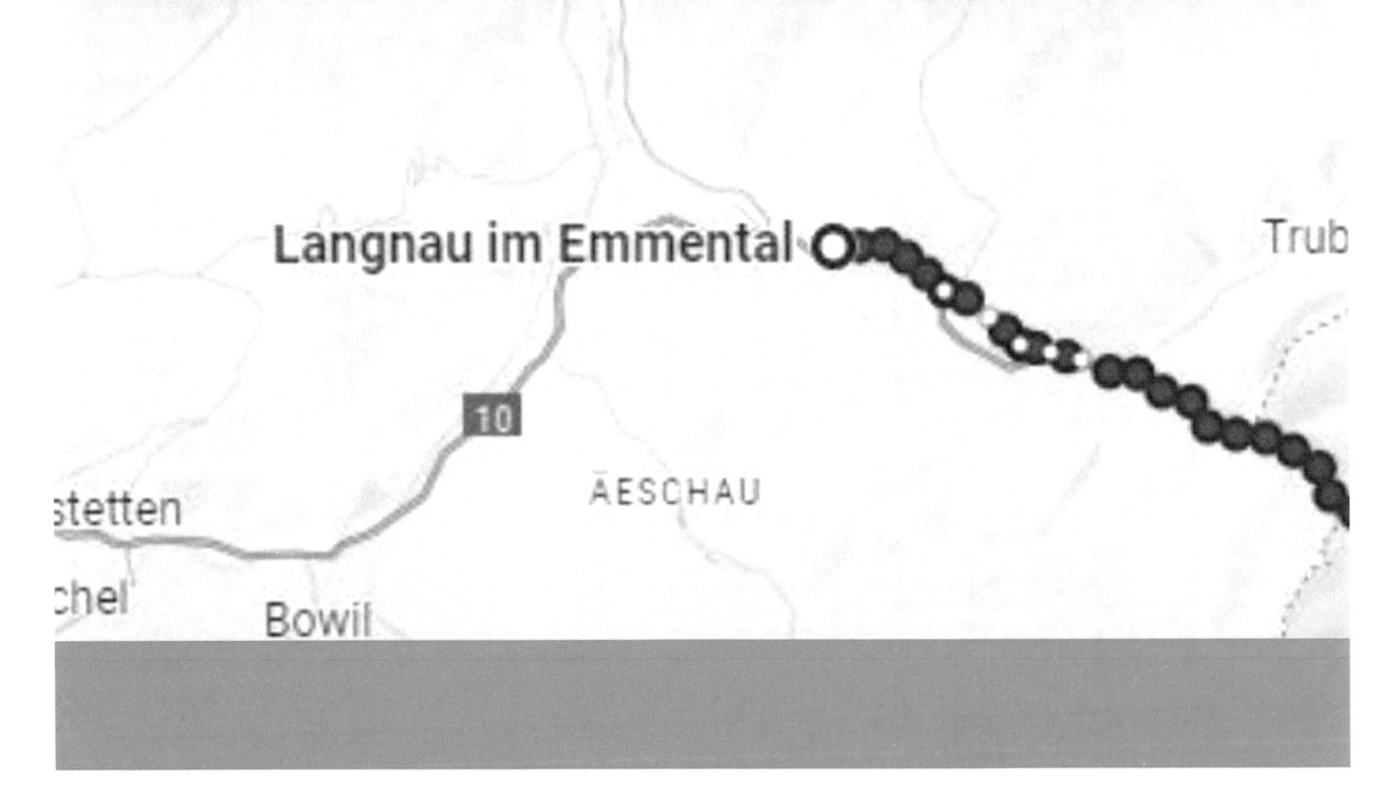

SCAN HERE

HOW TO USE QR CODE

- Open your phone's camera app or download scanner app from play store or apple store
- Point the camera at the QR code for a few seconds (no need to take a photo).
- A link should appear on the display, leading you to the location of the code

Sumiswald

SCAN HERE

HOW TO USE QR CODE

- Open your phone's camera app or download scanner app from play store or apple store
- Point the camera at the QR code for a few seconds (no need to take a photo).
- A link should appear on the display, leading you to the location of the code

Val Müstair

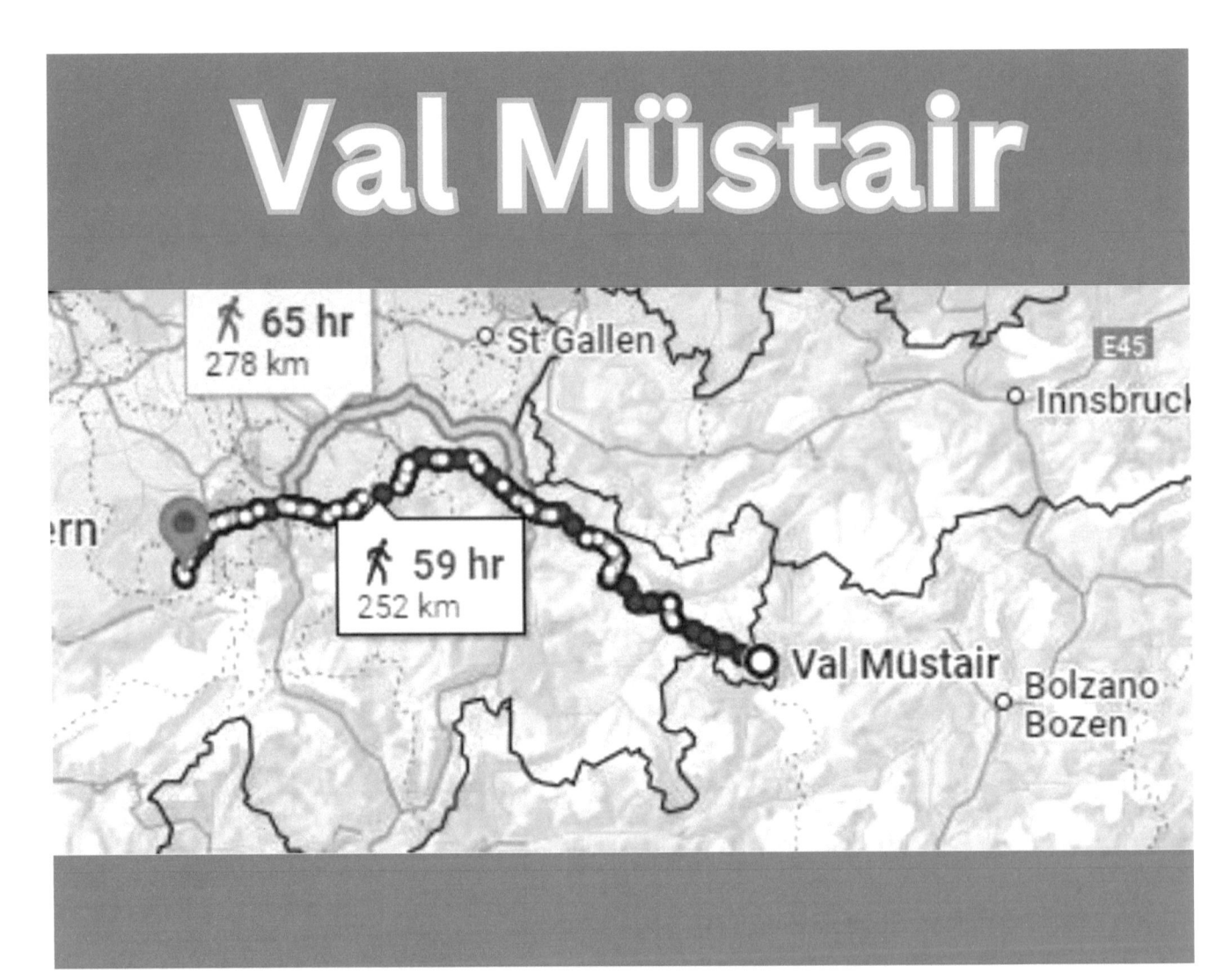

SCAN HERE

HOW TO USE QR CODE

- Open your phone's camera app or download scanner app from play store or apple store
- Point the camera at the QR code for a few seconds (no need to take a photo).
- A link should appear on the display, leading you to the location of the code

Zernez

SCAN HERE

HOW TO USE QR CODE

- Open your phone's camera app or download scanner app from play store or apple store
- Point the camera at the QR code for a few seconds (no need to take a photo).
- A link should appear on the display, leading you to the location of the code

Müstair

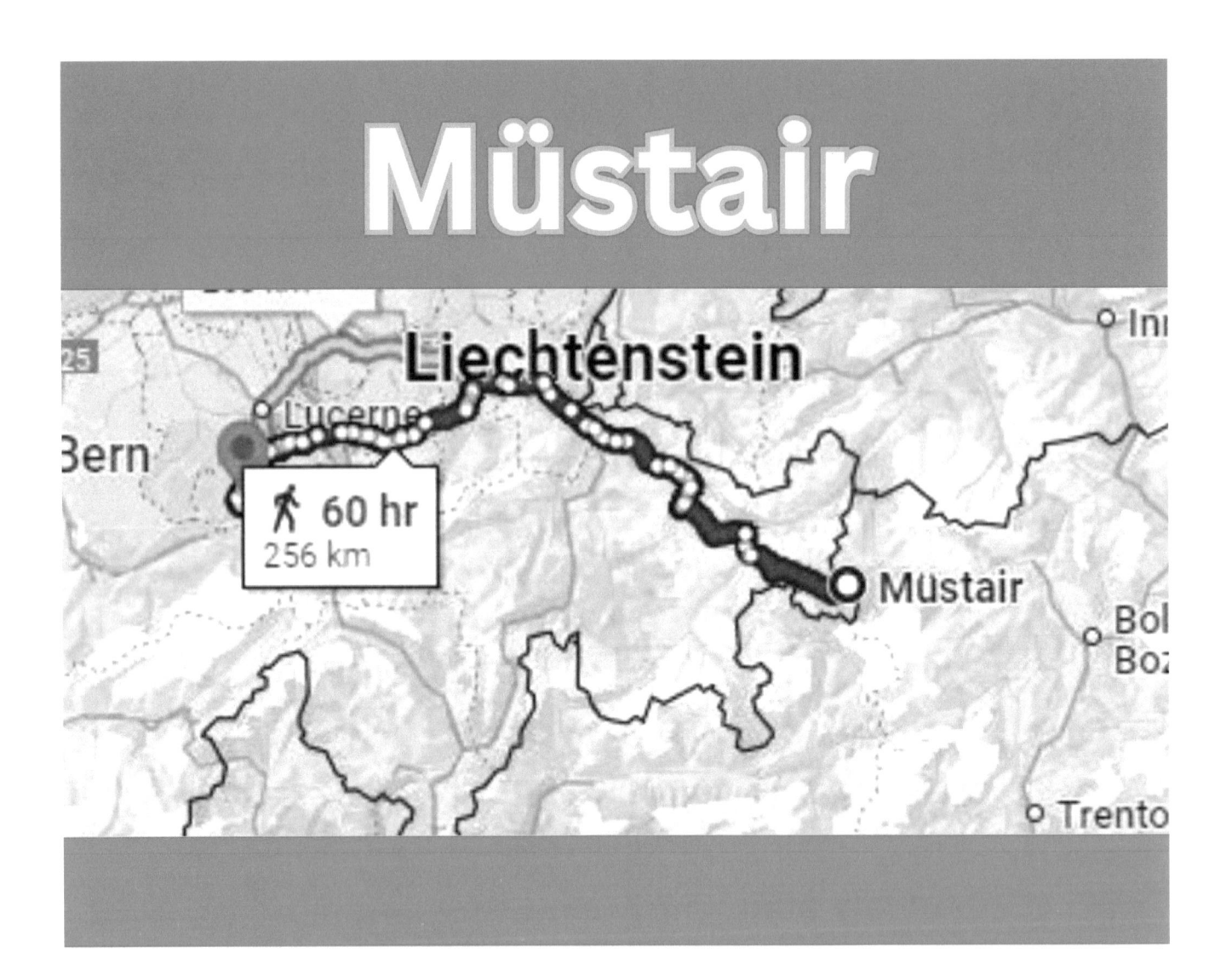

[Map showing route from Bern/Lucerne through Liechtenstein to Müstair: 60 hr, 256 km]

SCAN HERE   HOW TO USE QR CODE

- Open your phone's camera app or download scanner app from play store or apple store
- Point the camera at the QR code for a few seconds (no need to take a photo).
- A link should appear on the display, leading you to the location of the code

Swiss National Park

Convent of St. John Müstair

Jaun Pass

Boltigen

SCAN HERE

HOW TO USE QR CODE

- Open your phone's camera app or download scanner app from play store or apple store
- Point the camera at the QR code for a few seconds (no need to take a photo).
- A link should appear on the display, leading you to the location of the code

Jaun

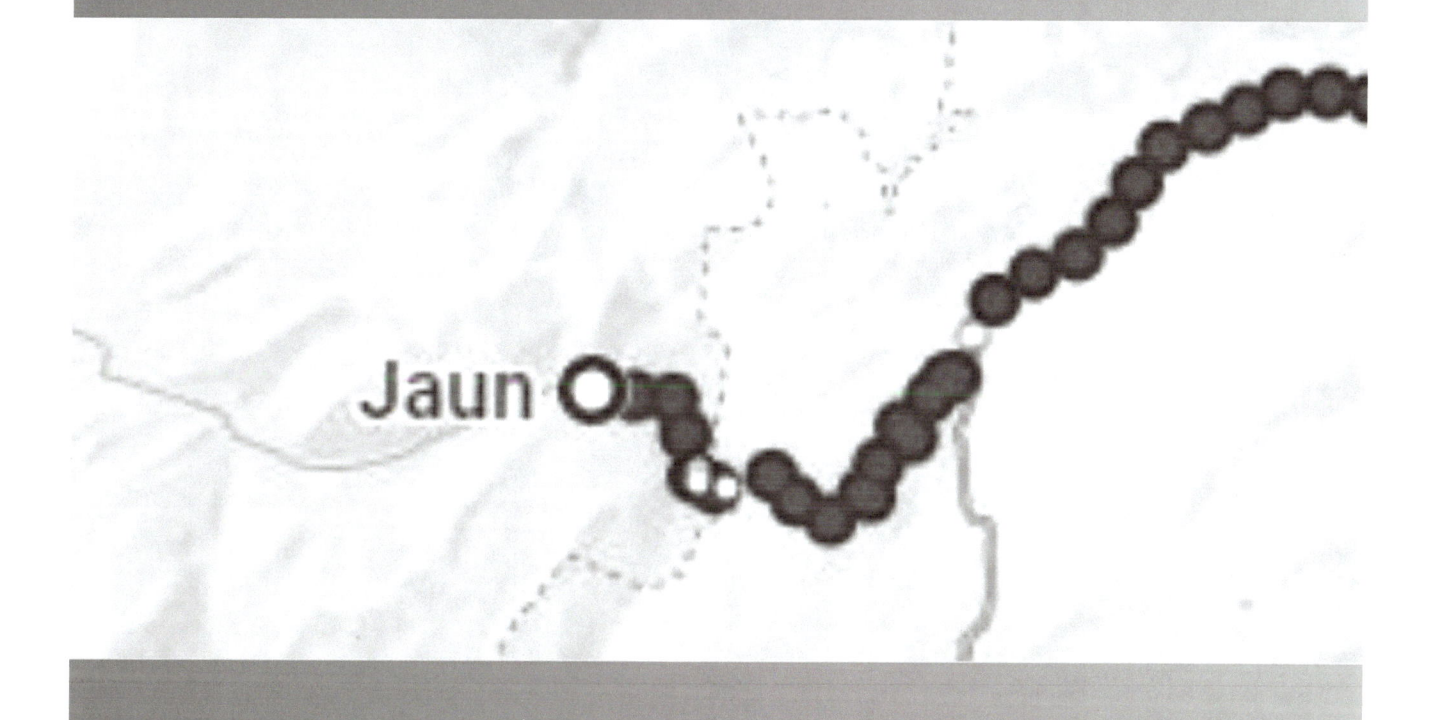

SCAN HERE

HOW TO USE QR CODE

- Open your phone's camera app or download scanner app from play store or apple store
- Point the camera at the QR code for a few seconds (no need to take a photo).
- A link should appear on the display, leading you to the location of the code

Waterfall at Jaun

Guarda

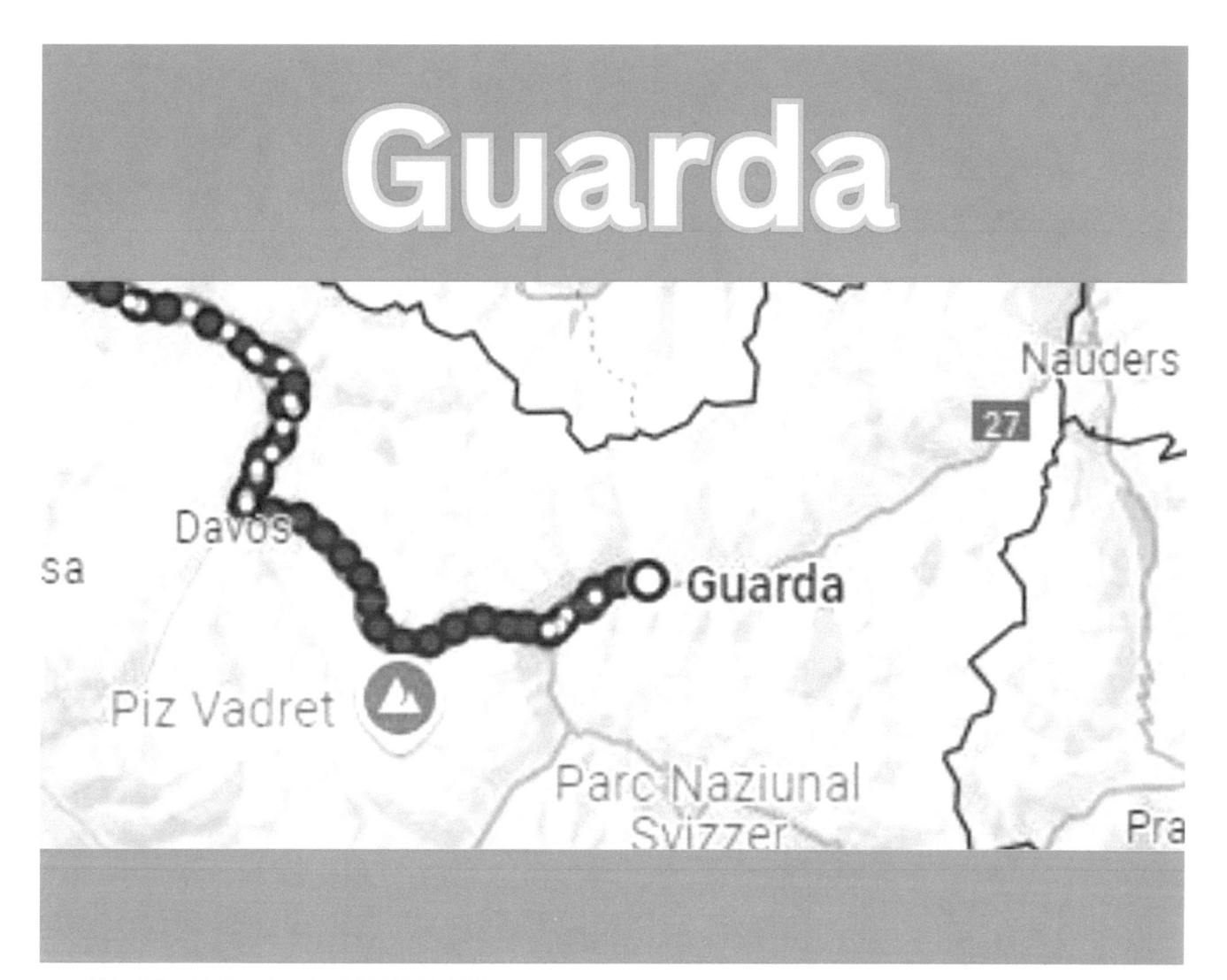

SCAN HERE

HOW TO USE QR CODE

- Open your phone's camera app or download scanner app from play store or apple store
- Point the camera at the QR code for a few seconds (no need to take a photo).
- A link should appear on the display, leading you to the location of the code

Iseltwald

Map showing Iseltwald, Niederried bei Interlaken

SCAN HERE

HOW TO USE QR CODE

- Open your phone's camera app or download scanner app from play store or apple store
- Point the camera at the QR code for a few seconds (no need to take a photo).
- A link should appear on the display, leading you to the location of the code

Lake Brienz

Lavertezzo

SCAN HERE

HOW TO USE QR CODE

- Open your phone's camera app or download scanner app from play store or apple store
- Point the camera at the QR code for a few seconds (no need to take a photo).
- A link should appear on the display, leading you to the location of the code

Lugano Farmers' Market

Vevey Market

Hotel Rosenlaui

Mont Chasseral

Lindt Chocolate Shop Verkehrshaus

Chapter 7

Driving Laws & Regulations for 2025

Navigating Switzerland's roads requires an understanding of the country's driving laws and regulations, especially with updates effective from 2025. These are essential information on new traffic rules, border crossing procedures, speed enforcement, parking regulations, and city specific restrictions to ensure a safe and compliant driving experience.

New Traffic Rules for 2025

Automated Driving

Starting in March 2025 Switzerland permits the use of self-driving technology on motorways. Drivers can engage automated systems and release the steering wheel; however, they must remain attentive and ready to assume control if necessary.

SWISSINFO.CH

Noise Regulations

To combat noise pollution stricter regulations have been implemented. Drivers are required to minimize avoidable noise, such as excessive engine revving and the use of loud exhaust systems. Non-compliance can result in significant fines.

MOBILITY-360.CH

Human-Powered Mobility

Regulations for human-powered vehicles, including bicycles and e-scooters, have been harmonized to enhance safety and integration with motorized traffic. Drivers should be aware of these changes to ensure respectful sharing of roadways.

MOBILITY-360.CH

Border Crossings & International Driving Rules

Border Crossings

Switzerland shares its borders with several countries: France, Germany, Italy, Austria, and Liechtenstein. As a traveler, understanding the procedures and regulations for crossing these borders is essential for a smooth journey.

1. Custom Regulations: Switzerland is not part of the European Union (EU), so customs regulations apply. Be aware of restrictions on certain goods, such as alcohol, tobacco, and firearms. Always check the latest customs allowances to avoid any surprises.

2. Identification: Ensure you carry a valid passport or national ID card when crossing borders. For EU citizens, an ID card is sufficient, whereas travelers from other countries may require a passport.

3. Border Control: While many borders are open without fixed checkpoints, expect to encounter border controls, especially during busy travel seasons. Always be ready for potential checks, which can include vehicle inspections and documentation verification.

4. Traveling with Children: If traveling with minors, ensure you have all necessary documentation, including consent forms from parents or guardians if not traveling with them. This is particularly relevant when crossing borders with a single parent or guardian.

International Driving Rules

1. Documentation: Carry a valid passport, driver license, vehicle registration, and proof of insurance.

2. International Driving Permit IDP: While Switzerland recognizes foreign licenses, some neighboring countries may require an IDP. Verify specific requirements before travel.

3. Vignettes and Tolls: Switzerland and Austria require a motorway vignette (toll sticker). France and Italy operate toll systems based on distance traveled. Ensure you have the appropriate vignette or means to pay tolls.

4. Equipment Requirements: Each country has specific requirements (e.g., safety vests, warning triangles). Familiarize yourself with and comply with these regulations.

5. Traffic Laws: Speed limits, alcohol tolerance, and other traffic laws vary by country. Research and adhere to each nation's regulations to avoid fines.

6. Traffic Laws: Switzerland adheres to strict traffic laws. Seat belts are mandatory for all passengers, and using a mobile phone while driving is prohibited unless hands-free. Speed limits are rigorously enforced, and fines can be steep.

Speed Cameras & Fines

In Switzerland, the enforcement of speed limits is strict, with a comprehensive network of speed cameras deployed across the country. These cameras serve as a deterrent against speeding, ensuring the safety of all road users. Understanding the system of speed cameras and the fines associated with violations is crucial for both residents and visitors.

Types of Speed Cameras

Fixed Speed Cameras: These are permanently installed in various locations, often in areas with a history of accidents or near schools and residential zones. They are strategically placed to monitor high-traffic areas and ensure compliance with speed limits.

Mobile Speed Cameras: Deployed by law enforcement, these cameras can be relocated and set up at different sites. Their mobile nature makes it difficult for drivers to anticipate their presence, encouraging adherence to speed limits throughout the country.

Speed Limits

- Motorways: 120 km/h
- Expressways: 100 km/h
- Outside built-up areas: 80 km/h
- Built-up areas: 50 km/h

Fines and Penalties

When a driver is caught speeding, the penalties can be significant. Fines vary based on the severity of the offense:

Minor Violations: Fines for exceeding the speed limit by a small margin (e.g., 1-5 km/h) may start at around CHF 40.

Moderate Violations: Exceeding the limit by larger margins can lead to fines ranging from CHF 100 to CHF 600, depending on how excessive the violation is.

Severe Violations: In cases of extreme speeding (above 25 km/h over the limit), the driver may face fines starting at CHF 600, possible license suspension, and even criminal charges in egregious cases.

Tips for Drivers

Stay Informed: Always be aware of the posted speed limits, as they can change frequently.

Observe the Signs: Pay attention to warning signs indicating speed camera locations or changing speed limits.

Utilize Technology: Consider using GPS systems or apps that provide real-time information about speed limits and camera locations.

Parking Laws & City Restrictions

Cities reflect this cultural ethos. Understanding these laws is essential for both residents and visitors to ensure compliance and avoid fines.

General Parking Regulations

Parking Zones: Most Swiss cities employ a color coded parking zone system. Areas marked in blue indicate paid parking, while white zones often signify free parking (usually subject to time limits). Yellow zones typically restrict parking for residents or specific permit holders.

Parking Fees: In urban areas, parking is often regulated by time and is subject to fees. Parking meters or machines are commonly found, and payments can usually be made via cash or credit card. Some cities also offer mobile payment options.

Time Limits: Many public parking areas have strict time limits, which may range from one hour to several hours. Always check the signage to avoid penalties.

City-Specific Regulations

1. Zurich: The city has extensive parking regulations. Parking spaces are available in garages and designated street areas. Residents require special permits to park their vehicles in specified zones.

2. Geneva: Similar to Zurich, Geneva has blue and white parking zones. The city promotes parking garages to manage space efficiently. Pay attention to the duration-free parking in designated areas, and be mindful of peak hours where restrictions may apply.

3. Bern: In Bern parking regulations vary by district. The center offers various parking options, but extended parking permits are required for residents. Visitors should utilize public transport whenever possible, as parking can be limited.

4. Lausanne: This hilly city has unique parking challenges. It's advisable to use the underground parking garages, as street parking is limited. Again, be aware of time restrictions in blue zones.

Special Considerations

Handicapped Parking: Spaces are designated for individual with disabilities, marked with signs. These spots often require a special permit. Visitors should ensure they have the appropriate documentation.

Loading Zones: Specific areas are designated for loading and unloading and are typically time restricted.

Staying informed about these regulations will help ensure a safe and lawful driving experience in Switzerland and its neighboring countries.

Susten Pass

Chapter 8

Conclusion

Final Tips for an Unforgettable Swiss Road Trip

Switzerland is one of the most spectacular destinations in the world for road trips. With its breathtaking alpine scenery, charming villages, and impeccably maintained roads, driving through this country is an experience like no other. To make the most of your Swiss road trip, here are some final tips, recommendations, and resources to ensure a smooth, memorable, and responsible journey.

Making the Most of Your Journey

A Swiss road trip isn't just about getting from point A to point B it's about the experiences along the way. Here are some ways to enhance your adventure:

Best Photography Spots

Switzerland is a photographer's paradise. Whether you're capturing majestic mountains, mirror-like lakes, or historic towns, you'll want to stop frequently to take it all in. Here are some must-visit photography locations:

The Matterhorn (Zermatt): One of the most iconic peaks in the world, best viewed at sunrise or sunset.

Lauterbrunnen Valley: A dreamy valley with waterfalls and picturesque Swiss chalets.

The Furka Pass: A winding mountain pass with incredible views, featured in James Bond's Goldfinger.

Lake Geneva (Lavaux Vineyards): A UNESCO-listed wine region with stunning terraces overlooking the lake.

Oeschinen Lake: A glacial lake with an unreal blue color, perfect for nature photography.

Château de Chillon (Montreux): A historic castle on the shores of Lake Geneva, offering fairy-tale-like scenery.

Appenzell & Aescher Cliff Restaurant: A small village known for its traditional Swiss culture and a famous cliffside restaurant.

Best Picnic Areas

Switzerland has countless scenic spots for a roadside picnic. Many rest stops along highways offer picnic tables with panoramic views. Here are some ideal locations:

Harder Kulm (Interlaken): A spectacular viewpoint with tables overlooking lakes and mountains.

Blausee (Blue Lake): A crystal-clear lake surrounded by dense forests, perfect for a peaceful lunch.

Lake Lucerne (Seelisberg): A quiet area above the lake with stunning views.

Emmental Valley: Rolling green hills famous for Swiss cheese, where you can find scenic picnic spots.

Val Verzasca (Ticino): A turquoise river with smooth rock formations, ideal for a summer picnic.

Unforgettable Memories

A Swiss road trip is filled with moments that will stay with you forever. Here are some ideas to make your journey even more special:

Take a scenic train ride: Even though you're on a road trip, a ride on the Glacier Express or Bernina Express offers a different perspective of Switzerland's landscapes.

Attend a local festival: If you visit in autumn, don't miss the Alpabzug, when cows are paraded down from mountain pastures in traditional decorations.

Stay in a mountain hut: Spending a night in a remote Berghotel (mountain hotel) offers an unforgettable alpine experience.

Try Swiss fondue with a view: Enjoy a traditional cheese fondue while looking out over the Swiss Alps.

Drive at sunrise or sunset: The golden light on Swiss peaks during these hours makes for magical driving moments.

A Note on Responsible Travel

Switzerland's natural beauty is one of its greatest treasures, and every traveler plays a role in preserving it. Here's how you can be a responsible road tripper:

- **Respecting Nature**

Follow the Leave No Trace principle: Take all trash with you and avoid disturbing wildlife.

Stick to marked roads: Off road driving is prohibited in Switzerland to protect the environment.

Choose eco friendly activities: Opt for hiking, biking and low impact tourism experiences.

- **Respecting Local Culture**

Greet locals with respect: A simple "Grüezi" (Swiss German), "Bonjour" (French), or "Buongiorno" (Italian) goes a long way.

Be mindful of noise: Swiss towns and countryside are known for their tranquility, so avoid unnecessary honking and loud music.

Respect rural traditions: If you're driving through farming regions, be patient with slow-moving vehicles or cattle crossings.

- **Road Etiquette**

Use designated parking areas: Avoid parking in undesignated spots, especially in nature reserves.

Yield on narrow roads: On mountain roads, uphill traffic generally has the right of way.

Drive responsibly in tunnels: Keep headlights on and maintain a steady speed.

Resources & Further Reading

For the most up-to-date information on road conditions, weather forecasts, and travel tips, here are some useful resources:

Official Swiss Travel & Road Information

Switzerland Tourism – www.myswitzerland.com

Swiss Federal Roads Office (ASTRA) – www.astra.admin.ch

Swiss Traffic Information (TCS) – www.tcs.ch

Swiss Weather Updates – www.meteoswiss.ch

Navigation & Route Planning Apps

Google Maps: Best for general navigation.

SBB Mobile: If you plan to combine driving with public transport.

ViaMichelin: Provides scenic route options and road trip planning.

Swisstopo: Switzerland's official map for detailed road and hiking routes.

Park4Night: Great for finding parking spots, especially for camper vans.

Swiss Driving & Rental Car Information

Automobile Club of Switzerland (ACS) – www.acs.ch

Swiss Vignette (Motorway Toll Sticker) – www.e-vignette.ch

Major Car Rental Companies – Hertz, Europcar, Avis, and Sixt all operate in Switzerland.

A road trip through Switzerland is one of the most rewarding travel experiences you can have. Whether you're winding through the high mountain passes, stopping for a picnic by a turquoise lake, or exploring medieval castles, every moment on the road offers something new and breathtaking.

With careful planning, respect for local customs, and an adventurous spirit, your Swiss road trip will be nothing short of unforgettable. So buckle up, embrace the journey, and enjoy every scenic mile!

Made in the USA
Thornton, CO
04/25/25 10:07:16

8fd65d7e-7a33-4d05-9793-b0419ac33259R01